IT'S ALL CHINESE TO ME

AN OVERVIEW OF CULTURE & ETIQUETTE IN CHINA

Pierre Ostrowski & Gwen Penner

TUTTLE PUBLISHING
Tokyo • Rutland, Vermont • Singapore

Published by Tuttle Publishing, an imprint of Periplus Editions (HK) Ltd., with editorial offices at 364 Innovation Drive, North Clarendon, Vermont 05759 U.S.A. and at 61 Tai Seng Avenue #02-12, Singapore 534167.

Library of Congress Cataloging-in-Publication Data

Ostrowski, Pierre, 1964-
    It's all Chinese to Me : an overview of culture & etiquette in China / Pierre Ostrowski & Gwen Penner. -- 1st ed.
       p. cm.
    Includes bibliographical references and index.
    ISBN 978-0-8048-4079-8 (pbk. : alk. paper)
1. Ethnology--China. 2. Business anthropology--China. 3. National characteristics, Chinese. 4. Cross-cultural orientation--China. 5. Culture shock--China. 6. Etiquette--China. 7. Rites and ceremonies--China.. 8. China--Social life and customs. I. Penner, Gwen, 1963- II. Title.
    GN635.C5O68 2009
    306.0951--dc22
                                            2009013153
ISBN 978-0-8048-4079-8

Distributed by

North America, Latin America & Europe
Tuttle Publishing
364 Innovation Drive
North Clarendon, VT 05759-9436 U.S.A.
Tel: 1 (802) 773-8930; Fax: 1 (802) 773-6993
info@tuttlepublishing.com
www.tuttlepublishing.com

Asia Pacific
Berkeley Books Pte. Ltd.
61 Tai Seng Avenue #02-12
Singapore 534167
Tel: (65) 6280-1330; Fax: (65) 6280-6290
inquiries@periplus.com.sg
www.periplus.com

First edition
14 13 12 11 10 09   10 9 8 7 6 5 4 3 2 1

Printed in Singapore

TUTTLE PUBLISHING® is a registered trademark of Tuttle Publishing, a division of Periplus Editions (HK) Ltd.

This book is dedicated to Suzanne, our long time
travel buddy and fellow lover of xiao long bao.
Sammy You!

Contents

Acknowledgments

First we would like to express our gratitude to our editor Virginia Freynet for her generous support and assistance. We would also like to thank all of our friends who provided wonderful insight about Chinese culture over the years. In particular, we would like to say thanks to Jean, Vicky and Charlie. Also, our heartfelt appreciation goes out to Sandra for her views on Buddhism and her wonderful lessons in Chinese cuisine. Finally, many thanks to all of our students over the years who provided us with invaluable insights into what it means to be Chinese.

Introduction

In recent times, many people in Western countries have become quite taken with China and all things Chinese. Aspects of Chinese culture like martial arts, feng shui and the Chinese language are rapidly gaining popularity and are becoming absorbed into mainstream Western culture. More and more manufacturers are shifting operations to China in order to take advantage of cheap and plentiful labor. It seems almost everything you buy these days has a "Made in China" sticker on it. The number of interactions between Westerners and Chinese is increasing exponentially. This has not always been the case.

For thousands of years, China has been a source of both mystery and fascination for the rest of the world. Geographically isolated and generally not interested in events outside its borders, China developed within its own set of unique social and cultural values. It has only been since the early 1980s that China has truly opened up to the outside world. Since that time, the country has undergone enormous changes. Indeed, it is fair to say that China has undergone more social and cultural changes in the last three decades than in its entire 4,000-year history.

One of the biggest changes in recent times is the opening of the economy to foreign investment beginning in the early 1980s. Before that time, China was all but cut off from the global economy. Since it has opened up, hundreds of foreign-owned companies have invested billions of dollars doing business in China. The number of these companies is growing rapidly. As the number of companies doing business in China grows, so too does the number of interpersonal interactions. Within these interactions are countless opportunities for misunderstandings based on cultural differences.

Cultural differences between East and West abound. First, Western societies tend to be multicultural. Within these societies, various ethnic groups are integrated and generally free to maintain their unique characteristics. China, on the other hand, is for the most part a homogeneous society. True, there are 55 recognized ethnic minority groups in China, totaling almost 100 million people. But in a country of over 1.3 billion, this number is a mere drop in the bucket. Furthermore, Chinese domestic policies toward minorities are more assimilative than integrative. Thus homogeneity rather than diversity is a fundamental goal.

Another factor separating China from the West is the difference in languages. Chinese is possibly the most difficult language in the world. Generally, Western languages are phonetic. This means they have alphabets, which are used to make various sounds according to specific rules of spelling. Chinese, however, is a pictographic language.

Chinese words, called characters, are essentially pictures. Each character represents a word that can be used in combination with one or more other characters to form compound words. There are over 65,000 characters and the only way to know them is through memorization; a well-educated Chinese person today recognizes about 6,000 to 7,000 characters. Unlike English and other phonetic languages, if you come across a new word while reading Chinese, it is not possible to sound out the word by looking at letters. Either you know a character or you don't. There is no middle ground.

Finally, one of the biggest contributors to cultural variations is related to historical differences. When comparing Chinese and Western cultures, it is crucial to be aware of the almost total lack of shared history. Throughout the ages, China was more or less cut off from developments in the Western world. Some of the Western developments that bypassed China over the centuries include the Greek and Roman empires, Christianity, the Age of Discovery, the Renaissance, the Industrial Revolution and the Scientific Revolution. These all played crucial roles in shaping Western values, yet had very little impact on Chinese thinking.

More recently, there are countless historical incidences which had absolutely no impact for the average Chinese person while they were occurring. These include things like jazz, rock and roll, the Kennedy assassinations, the 1960s, etc. Historically, Western nations have very little in common with China regarding social and cultural movements. This lack of shared history is a major source of differences in Chinese and Western thinking. Considering this together with differences in social makeup and linguistic differences, it is easy to see that bridging the gap between East and West is beset with a number of obstacles.

The expression "It's all Chinese to me" is a phrase used to express bewilderment or an inability to understand. The main purpose of this book is to dispel the sense of bafflement many Westerners feel when encountering Chinese people or when becoming immersed in Chinese culture. Our aim is to be as informative as possible about general differences and tendencies in Western and Chinese societies. We hope that by using illustrations and text we can provide a dynamic reading experience. As the saying goes, "A picture is worth a thousand words." We hope the experiential nature of the illustrations in this book can serve to confirm this maxim.

Please note that this book is in no way an academic treatise on the "how's" and "why's" of a specific cultural aspect with a highly limited focus. Rather, and as the subtitle suggests, it is a very general and broad overview of China and its culture. With this in mind, it is important to remember that many of the observations in this book do not necessarily apply to every Chinese individual.

For every generalization made in this book, there will be countless individuals who don't fit the mold. Nevertheless, awareness of the major cultural differences between China and the West can serve to promote meaningful and mutually fulfilling relationships between these different regions of the world. Our wish in writing this book is to contribute favorably to this prospect.

CHINESE HISTORY
(CONDENSED VERSION)

Any attempt to sum up China's vast history in three pages or less is of course sheer folly. The following is merely a brief synopsis of two aspects of Chinese history that have proven instrumental in shaping modern China's views and attitudes toward the outside world. The main focus is on the effects of China's imperial past as well as on the consequences of foreign imperialism in shaping the Chinese worldview on global relations.

Imperial China

With a history dating back over 4,000 years, China is widely considered the world's longest continuous civilization. Throughout much of that time, China was essentially closed off from the outside world. This was by and large a deliberate state of affairs on China's part owing to its relatively advanced level of development in comparison to the rest of the world.

In the first millennium CE, while Europe was toiling under the yoke of a decaying Roman Empire and muddling its way through the Dark Ages, China was arguably the most technologically and economically developed empire on the face of the earth. As far as China was concerned, the rest of the world was nothing but an insignificant collection of assorted barbarians with absolutely nothing to offer. Interaction with the outside world was all but meaningless— hence the building of the Great Wall to keep out the riffraff.

By the time Marco Polo made his way to the Far East in the late 13th century, China was a highly sophisticated, well-organized and technologically advanced empire in its own right. The Chinese word for "China" is *Zhong Guo*. This term literally means "Central Nation" but is usually translated as " Middle Kingdom." The implication of this name is that the Chinese have, for thousands of years, considered their nation to be the center of the world. The primary purpose of all other nations outside its borders was to pay tribute and to serve as vassal states to the great empire.

It is important to note that the vast majority of Chinese people today are keenly aware of their illustrious and glorious past. It is a fundamental source of national pride and contributes greatly to what can best be termed a sense of cultural superiority to the rest of the world. To put it in context, imagine the sense of pride and superiority Americans would feel if, in 4,000 years from now, their nation was still in existence and was still a global military and economic power. In today's re-emerging "Middle Kingdom," fervent nationalism and a strong sense of cultural superiority are two powerful undercurrents that flow through China's consciousness.

Some notable Chinese inventions indicative of cultural and technological advancement include these:

Noodles: circa 2,000 BCE
The crossbow: 4th century BCE
The catapult: 4th century BCE
Papermaking: 100 CE
Gunpowder: 142 CE
The magnetic compass: 11th century CE
Movable type printing: 1040 CE
Ice cream: 11th century CE
The cannon: 12th century CE
Restaurants: 12th century CE

China: The oldest civilization in the world with over 4,000 years of uninterrupted history.

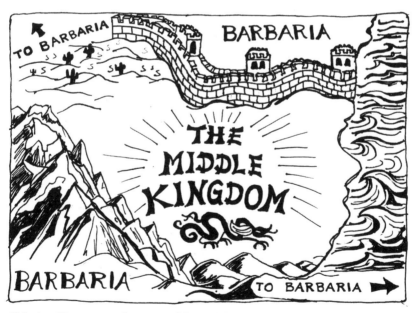

China's self concept as the center of the world as evidenced by its name *Zhong Guo*; literally this means "Central Nation" but it's commonly translated as "The Middle Kingdom."

Four Great Inventions of Ancient China

Papermaking—100 CE

Gunpowder—142 CE

THE COMPASS WAS INVENTED IN CHINA IN THE 11TH CENTURY IT WAS USED FIRST AS A TOOL IN FENG SHUI.

The Magnetic Compass—11th century CE

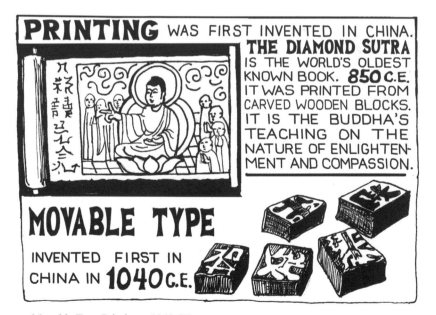

PRINTING WAS FIRST INVENTED IN CHINA. THE DIAMOND SUTRA IS THE WORLD'S OLDEST KNOWN BOOK. 850 C.E. IT WAS PRINTED FROM CARVED WOODEN BLOCKS. IT IS THE BUDDHA'S TEACHING ON THE NATURE OF ENLIGHTENMENT AND COMPASSION.

MOVABLE TYPE INVENTED FIRST IN CHINA IN 1040 C.E.

Movable Type Printing—1040 CE

End of the Empire

In the mid-19th century, China's position as the impregnable center of the universe came under serious threat from the outside world. Thousands of years of isolation had led to social, political and economic stagnation. Completely insulated from pivotal developments in Europe and elsewhere, most notably the Scientific and Industrial Revolutions (18th and 19th centuries), China's longstanding technological and economic supremacy relative to the rest of the world no longer held sway.

In the 1850s, with the help of some of China's very own inventions (i.e., the magnetic compass, gunpowder and the cannon) Great Britain defeated China in the first of many foreign-initiated wars. The result was the forceful opening of China's borders to foreign trade for the first time in history. Subsequently, a great many other foreign powers, including Japan, France, Russia, the U.S.A. and several more, joined in to grab their share of the pie and carve out their own spheres of influence. By 1911, the great Chinese Empire was no more and the country fragmented into a loose confederation of regions ruled by warlords and gangsters. This situation prevailed until the communist takeover in 1949.

Imperial China's defeat at the hands of foreign "barbarians" was a humiliation of unprecedented scale. It led to at least a century of political and economic instability with enormous suffering and hardship for the masses. Again it must be noted that Chinese people are keenly aware of this period in history. Consequently, their perception of the outside world is tainted with strong feelings of mistrust and suspicion. Furthermore, the humiliating nature of China's historic capitulation to foreign outsiders fosters feelings of dishonor that undermine otherwise significant feelings of national pride.

Conclusion

To sum up, China's long history as an invincible empire together with its more recent history as a victim of foreign imperialism has shaped the Chinese worldview in two fundamental ways. Chinese attitudes in foreign relations can be characterized as consisting of feelings of cultural superiority coupled with contradictory feelings of technological inferiority. Whereas there is a certain amount of respect for Western accomplishments in technology, there is also condescension toward the West due to its seeming lack of cultural development. In addition, there are also feelings of animosity and distrust.

The period of great humiliation: The carving up of Imperial China by foreign "barbarian" nations (mid-19th–mid-20th century CE).

2

POLITICS AND SOCIETY

With a population now estimated at about 1.3 billion, one of the first things you will notice in China are the crowded conditions—particularly in the cities. "People Mountain People Sea" is a Chinese idiom, which basically means "Very Crowded."

Booming China: A Highly Localized Phenomenon

In 1978, Deng Xiaoping, the de facto leader of China at that time, proclaimed: "To get rich is glorious." Since then, China has moved rapidly from a centrally planned economy to a market economy. In doing so, China has undergone enormous social change resulting in a rapidly growing middle class. Most of the prosperity has emerged in the larger cities in Eastern China. In the countryside, however, prosperity has been much slower in coming.

As a result, there are now essentially two Chinas:

1. The increasingly prosperous and modern urban centers such as Beijing, Shanghai and Hong Kong (roughly 350–400 million people; about 30% of China's total population)
and
2. The rest of China (roughly 900–950 million people; about 70% of China's total population). This group is by far the largest segment of society and lives mostly in the countryside. Unlike their rich urban cousins, this group of rural peasants generally lives in a state of chronic, absolute poverty.

Fundamentally, China's economic boom is highly localized and is not a truly national phenomenon. The inequitable distribution of wealth being generated by China's present economic boom is perhaps the greatest challenge currently facing the Chinese people. Unless properly addressed, it is a huge potential source of political instability.

Emerging Problems

Crushing poverty in the countryside and disproportionate wealth in the cities has created a number of problems for China's major metropolises. In the last four decades, China has seen a massive increase in internal migration. Huge numbers of people continue to relocate to the cities in search of jobs. Consequently, China's major cities tend to be severely overcrowded. Traffic jams, housing shortages and pollution problems are all a part of daily life in urban China.

The emergence of a sizable urban middle class is also bringing about considerable changes to Chinese family life. There is an obvious generation gap forming between China's internet-savvy urban youth and the older generations raised on Maoist propaganda. Much to the dismay of their elders, many hip young Chinese people are increasingly rejecting traditional values and adopt-

In modern urban China, many people aspire to acquiring material wealth in the form of electronic goods, new cars and beautiful homes—very much like their Western counterparts.

In the countryside, the vast majority of people, over 900 million peasants, are mostly concerned with having enough rice for their next meal. Most of China is dirt poor.

ing Western ways. This is a major potential source for dramatic social change in the future.

Another potential source of social change in China is the controversial One-Child Policy. In an effort to keep its population growth under control, the Chinese government began implementing a national birth control program in the early 1980s. Under this program, couples that have more than one child in urban areas are required to pay a "social compensation fee"—essentially a fine. In rural areas and depending on the various provincial governments, the policy is sometimes less rigid. Couples are in many cases allowed to have two children depending on their circumstances.

One problem related to the One-Child Policy is associated with the Chinese preference for having a son over having a daughter. In rural areas, sons are generally seen as more valuable because of their potential to contribute to farm work. Also, in both rural and urban areas, sons are generally expected to support the parents in their retirement.

Limited to having only one child, some couples allegedly resort to drastic measures in order to ensure that their only child is male. These measures, despite being illegal in China, apparently include female infanticide, gender-selected abortion using ultrasound and also female child abandonment. The British Parliament, the U.S. State Department and Amnesty International have all

In Chinese society, a significant generation gap is forming between the conservative, older generation and the technology-savvy, younger generation. How this situation will affect China's future development remains to be seen.

In an effort to control population growth, China implemented a birth control program that uses financial penalties to discourage couples from having more than one child—the so-called "One-Child Policy." Billboards like the one illustrated above as well as other forms of media campaigns designed to limit family size abound throughout China.

China's overcrowded urban jungles.

China's ever-growing pollution problem.

concluded that China's One-Child Policy contributes to instances of female infanticide. Also, as recent as 2001, a report out of Guangdong province surfaced that revealed a quota of 20,000 forced abortions and sterilizations had been set for Huaiji County as a result of non-compliance to the government's birth control program. This occurred despite officially stated policies that outlaw such practices.

Currently in Mainland China, the gender ratio at birth (male to female) is 117:100. This is significantly higher than the natural baseline, which is around 103:100. According to China's State Population and Family Planning Commission, men will outnumber women by about 30 million in the year 2020. A massive shortage of wives is a likely prospect. This could eventually prove to be a significant source of social and political unrest in the imminent future.

Iron Fisted Rule

Politically, China is a one-party totalitarian state. Responsibility for maintaining control over China's vast population rests with the Chinese Communist Party (the CCP). The CCP maintains its grip on power mainly through the People's Liberation Army (the PLA). At present, the CCP's hold on power is absolute. Anyone dreaming of democracy sweeping over China any time soon should not hold their breath.

The Chinese legal system is the CCP's other means of social control. In China, justice is based on civil law rather than on common law as it is in Britain and North America. As such, judges in China function more as grand inquisitors rather than as impartial arbitrators. Furthermore, Chinese judges are under the direct supervision of the CCP. Therefore, legal decisions in China are ultimately political in nature. Justice is arbitrary and subject to the whims of political leaders in charge.

In China, "justice" is also swift and merciless. Capital punishment is meted out for a wide variety of crimes including embezzlement, auto theft and of course murder. With over 6,000 prisoners put to death every year, China is by far the world leader in state executions. The United States, by comparison, executes roughly 150 people per year. Furthermore, every year in China, countless criminal suspects mysteriously "fall" out of windows during police interrogations. In China, committing a crime or opposing a local government official can often prove fatal.

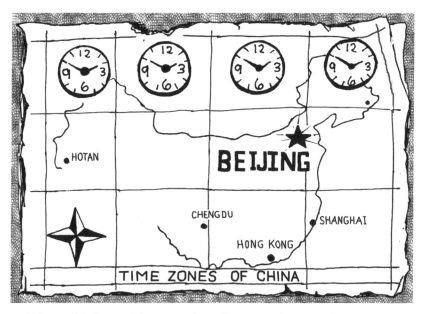

In China, political control is centered in Beijing. It lies in the hands of the Chinese Communist Party (the CCP). The CCP's grip on power is symbolized by the fact that all clocks in China are set to Beijing time—despite the fact that China covers four time zones.

The CCP enforces control over the nation primarily through the People's Liberation Army (the PLA). This was made abundantly clear at Tiananmen Square during the PLA crackdown on pro-democracy demonstrators in 1989. This show of force resulted in over 2,000 dead and scores more imprisoned.

Essentially a totalitarian state, China is in many ways a very secretive society. In certain circumstances you may find yourself being told to mind your own affairs.

Western judges are largely independent and expected to act as impartial arbitrators, much like referees. Chinese judges, on the other hand, are under the supervision of the CCP. They are expected to obey orders from their political leaders above.

The more regulations there are, the poorer people become.

—Lao Tzu

BLIND JUSTICE | POLITICAL POWER

Whereas many Western countries strive for the ideal of fair, balanced and blind justice (though not always successfully), justice in China is best represented by a set of shackles to be used by those in power when it suits their purpose.

Conclusion

In sum, China is a vast country beset with numerous challenges. With so many people to govern, simply maintaining order is the government's primary concern. The army and the legal system are the two principal mechanisms of social control. Within these branches of government, harsh measures are in place to keep people in line. Government justification for the use of excessive means in maintaining order is the argument that total chaos is a very real possibility in a country of over one billion people.

The probability of social and political instability in China is increasing every day as the gap between rich and poor continues to widen. Frustration amongst China's 900 to 950 million peasants living in abject poverty is growing. Sporadic demonstrations and riots crop up almost daily throughout the country. In times to come, expect the Chinese government to dig in and resort to increasingly harsh policies so as to maintain order and control.

3

🏛 MAJOR INFLUENCES IN CHINESE THOUGHT: TAOISM, BUDDHISM, CONFUCIANISM

Although China's political history goes back over 4,000 years, Chinese mythology goes back even further—some historians speculate perhaps 10,000 years or more. Nature gods were some of the first deities to be worshipped. One of the most important gods in Chinese tradition was a snake god that later evolved into a dragon god. Today, the dragon is the most well-known symbol of China's cultural identity. As the historical symbol of the Chinese emperor, it is considered a symbol of power and masculinity.

Over the centuries, three great systems of religious thought emerged and contributed greatly to the character of Chinese culture. They are Taoism, Buddhism and Confucianism. To this day, each one of these religions continues to exert considerable influence in Chinese society. It is interesting to note that all three of these religions began as philosophical systems. They were later transformed over time by their followers into systems of worship.

Though all three systems have their unique characteristics, followers of all three religions share one practice in common: ancestor worship, rooted in Confucianism. Furthermore, over the years, all three religions have borrowed and adopted various practices from one another. This has produced a uniquely Chinese religious blend. Buddhists and Taoists often worship each other's gods and both religions incorporate many concepts from Confucianism.

All three of China's religions are founded on the teachings of three great masters. Each master had his own unique philosophical approach to life. Taoism has its roots in the writings of noted sage Lao Tzu (circa 600–500 BCE). It emphasizes the central role Nature plays in maintaining harmony in the universe. Buddhism, based on the teachings of the Buddha (circa 563–483 BCE), focuses on eliminating earthly desire and living a life of compassion. Finally, Confucianism, based on the writings of Confucius (circa 551–479 BCE), is concerned mainly with teaching proper behavior as a means of attaining social harmony.

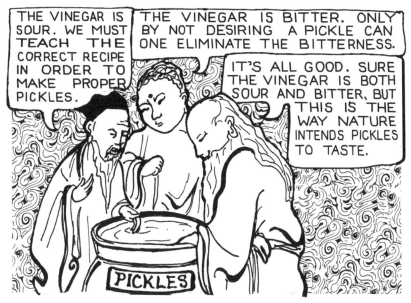

A well-known parable in China has Confucius, Buddha and Lao Tzu discussing the contents of a pickle jar. It illustrates quite well the different ways each one of these sages has influenced Chinese culture. The comment made by Confucius reflects the ideal of teaching proper behavior in order to achieve social harmony. Buddha's remark reflects the Buddhist principle of eliminating desire in order to achieve inner peace. Finally, Lao Tzu's statement reflects the Taoist notion of accepting Nature's pivotal role in shaping life and the Universe.

Taoism

Taoism, one of the foremost religions in Chinese society, was originally a philosophy with its roots in nature worship. At around 500 BCE, the sage Lao Tzu wrote *The Tao Te Ching*. In it, he proposed that the *Tao* or "the natural way to heaven" could be found by living in harmony with nature. Lao Tzu emphasized that knowledge can be gained by understanding the principles of nature as represented by "yin and yang."

According to Taoist thought, *yin* is the feminine side of nature. It is dark, cool, passive and soft. It represents the earth. *Yang* is the masculine side of nature. It is hot, bright, active and solid. It represents heaven. Everything in the universe contains both yin and yang. When existing in balance, yin and yang maintain the harmony of nature.

As a religion based in nature, Taoism includes animism. Because it is believed that all things in the universe possess a soul, Taoist temples are dedicated to a vast number of deities. These deities include nature gods, dragons, tigers and various mythical heroes. The highest Taoist deity is the Jade Emperor.

Another fundamental tenet of Taoism is the acceptance of the transitory nature of life. All things in the universe are in a constant state of flux. By accepting change as the only constant in life, one can flow in harmony with nature. In an attempt to exist in harmony with nature, Taoists are concerned with observing natural phenomena and seeking out the mysterious ebb and flow of the universe. As such, Taoism, as a philosophy, lends itself quite well to scientific observation as well as to artistic endeavors. Many of China's most famous poets, artists and inventors can trace the origins of their accomplishments to Taoist philosophy.

In modern China, Taoist influence permeates Chinese culture in a number of ways. Traditional Chinese medicine, such as acupuncture, is rooted in Taoist philosophy; so are Chinese fortune telling and the art of feng shui—the practice of aligning one's physical environment in harmony with nature.

Lessons from Nature: A basic tenet of Taoism stresses the never-ending ebb and flow of the universe. It is analogous to the flow of water. Water is soft and yielding but over time, it can dissolve even the tallest of mountains. Nothing is permanent.

Buddhism

Buddhism arrived in China between 50 BCE and 50 CE. The basic principle in Buddhism is that human suffering is the result of earthly desire. Eliminate desire, and you will achieve happiness. Buddhism has its roots in Hinduism. The Buddha, Siddhartha Gautama, was an Indian prince who gave up his earthly life to seek wisdom. After years of searching and through prolonged meditation, he transcended the earthly plane and became the Buddha or the "Enlightened One."

Buddhists believe in reincarnation. One's karma, the result of one's actions in past lives, determines what kind of existence one will have in the next life. The goal of Buddhism is to escape the endless cycle of death and rebirth. This can be accomplished by practicing compassion and by achieving enlightenment, thus entering Nirvana—an eternal state of peace where one is free from all desire.

In China, Buddhism is the largest organized faith with 300–350 million adherents. Not only is the Buddha worshipped, but a female incarnation of the Buddha called Guan Yin is also widely worshipped. She is the goddess of mercy and compassion and serves as a role model for many followers of Buddhism.

One of the more profound ways in which Buddhism influences Chinese society is reflected in the preponderance of Non-Governmental Charity Organizations (NGCOs) in China. Currently, there are over 280,000 NGCOs ministering to the needs of the less fortunate in China and elsewhere. One of the most famous charities, based in Taiwan, The Buddhist Compassion Relief Tzu Chi Foundation, has dozens of branches worldwide, with thousands of volunteers in over fifty countries. They provide schools, universities, hospitals, recycling programs and disaster relief to those in need. Altruism and compassion are two aspects of Buddhism that have a positive impact on the Chinese worldview.

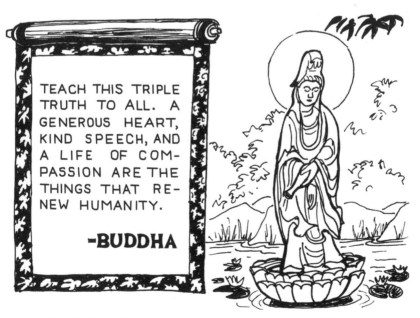

TEACH THIS TRIPLE TRUTH TO ALL. A GENEROUS HEART, KIND SPEECH, AND A LIFE OF COMPASSION ARE THE THINGS THAT RENEW HUMANITY.

-BUDDHA

Lessons from the Heart: Kindness, generosity and compassion for all living beings are the hallmarks of Buddhism. Kind-hearted people are plentiful throughout China.

Confucianism

Confucianism is a complex political, ethical, philosophical andreligious system. It is based on the teachings of Confucius (551–479 BCE). From around 100 BCE into the 20th century it has been perhaps the most important force shaping Chinese society. Over the millennia, Confucianism has had a profound impact on the nature of Chinese government and education. It has also had a profound influence on personal behavior within Chinese society.

At around 100 BCE, Emperor Wu of Han declared Confucianism to be China's official state philosophy. During the Tang Dynasty (618–907 CE), Confucianism lost its official sanction. Nevertheless, over the course of the last two millennia, it has remained the dominant orthodoxy in Chinese society. As a religion, it has no clergy and it does not address typical spiritual concerns such as human suffering and life after death. It is primarily a moral guide and a prescription for good government. Three of the most important ways in which Confucian thought continues to exert influence in Chinese society today are:

- A hierarchical approach to social organization.
- A heavy emphasis on scholarship.
- A focus away from the individual as the the unit of society and toward the family as the primary unit of social organization.

WITHOUT AN ACQUAINTANCE WITH THE RULES OF PROPRIETY, IT IS IMPOSSIBLE FOR THE CHARACTER TO BE ESTABLISHED. — Confucius

Lessons from Tradition: Confucianism, with its emphasis on striving for social harmony through proper conduct, has had enormous influence on Chinese society.

Confucian Influence #1: The Confucian Hierarchy

Confucius lived in an era of great social and political instability. His primary concern was to devise a way to bring about order and harmony in China. He believed that all people have a purpose and a station in society. Moreover, he believed that every station comes with a prescribed set of behaviors. If everyone understood their rank in society and were taught the proper behaviors conducive to their rank, then social harmony could be achieved.

Essentially, Confucian views on attaining social harmony can be summed up in the phrase "A place for everyone and everyone in their place." There is also the added condition that "Once in your place, you must behave in a way that befits your rank." Thus for example, a husband must act "husbandly" or a teacher must act "teacherly." Failure to act appropriately means you have not been taught well and are in need of remedial lessons in "proper behavior." One key aspect of this view is that "proper behavior" is defined externally by someone else and must be learned.

In devising his hierarchical approach to social organization, Confucius identified five cardinal relationships. They are:

1. Ruler to ruled.
2. Husband to wife.
3. Parents to children.
4. Older to younger siblings.
5. Friend to friend.

Within this organizational structure, the "rulers" are, in descending order: the government, husbands, parents and older brothers. The "ruled" are, in descending order: wives, children and younger brothers. Within this framework, the "ruled" freely give their obedience and loyalty to the "rulers" in exchange for benevolence on the part of their superiors.

Perhaps the most important impact of Confucian ideas on rank in Chinese society is that Chinese people tend to demonstrate a considerable amount of reverence for authority. In addition, it is imperative in Chinese culture to show proper respect and deference to one's elders or superiors. Often this respect is heartfelt and sincere, however, this is not always the case.

Even if one does not necessarily feel respectful to one's superiors, whatever the reason may be, in the interest of social harmony, it is still important to at least behave with reverence and obedience. Consequently, much of what is seen as social harmony in Chinese society is often merely surface harmony—a veneer of "proper behavior" but lacking any real sincerity.

In other words, Chinese people often act according to how they are supposed to act within their rank and not necessarily according to how they actually feel. For Westerners interacting with Chinese people, it is not always clear whether the Chinese really mean what they are saying or if they are merely following prescribed behavior patterns suitable to their station. This contributes greatly to the Western notion of the "inscrutable Chinese."

The five cardinal relationships as identified by Confucius: 1. Ruler to ruled; 2. Husband to wife; 3. Parents to children; 4. Older to younger siblings; 5. Friend to friend. These relationships are widely considered to form the basis of the Confucian hierarchy of social organization.

Confucian Influence #2: The Importance of Scholarship

Another important influence of Confucianism in Chinese society is its heavy emphasis on scholarship. As a means of organizing society, Confucius believed in the concept of eradicating hereditary rule by the aristocracy. Instead he favored rule based on scholarship and learning, i.e., a meritocracy. This eventually gave rise to the Imperial examination system of China (circa 605 CE).

Within the Imperial examination system, any male who studied hard enough to pass a series of extremely difficult exams could become a government official. This position came with considerable wealth and prestige. It meant working in a career dedicated to public service. In essence, the system gave rise to the world's first modern civil service.

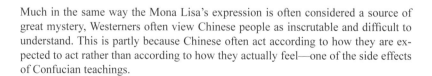

Much in the same way the Mona Lisa's expression is often considered a source of great mystery, Westerners often view Chinese people as inscrutable and difficult to understand. This is partly because Chinese often act according to how they are expected to act rather than according to how they actually feel—one of the side effects of Confucian teachings.

Social mobility through higher education was a key facet of ancient China. It meant any male with the right ability had a chance to rise above his social rank. Competition for government positions was fierce. The examination process was based entirely on rote memorization of Chinese classical literature and philosophy.

In modern China, social advancement through higher learning has much in common with the Imperial examination system. Entrance to prestigious universities is very limited due to China's enormous population. Also, to say that competition is fierce is an understatement. Finally, as in ancient times, much of the modern Chinese education system is still based on rote memorization. It is a system that leaves very little room for creative thought.

The Chinese Education System

The education system in China is still very much rooted in Confucian philosophy. Beginning in elementary school, children endure round after round of extremely stringent exams. Students dream of attaining high enough marks to advance academically and gain acceptance into prestigious schools. Tests are based primarily on rote memorization and students seldom have a chance to express themselves through written or oral presentations. There is very little opportunity for individual creativity. Achieving excellent grades year after year on a never-ending series of multiple-choice exams is the only thing most students worry about throughout their academic life.

In China, pressure to do well academically is intense. Given its massive population, competition for well-paying jobs exceeds anything the average Westerner can imagine. Parents in China go to great lengths to ensure the success of their children. Bribing school officials so one's child can gain entry into a prominent academic program is not unusual. Corporal punishment is also generally not frowned upon.

In many elementary and junior high schools, the school year begins in September with teachers sending notes home to the parents. These notes are permission slips to hit the children in the upcoming academic session. Very often, not only do parents grant their permission, but they also ask the teachers to provide "extra hitting." Teen suicide as a result of poor academic performance is not uncommon. Remarkably, getting a grade of 90% on an exam is, in many cases, considered a poor performance!

With its huge population, Chinese schools tend to be overcrowded and underfunded. Generally, classrooms have 50 to 60 students or more. Students and their families normally have to pay for tuition, books, school uniforms and meals. These meals consist primarily of rice and oily vegetables provided by local restaurants and snack shops.

Students typically arrive at school at about 7:00 or 7:30 AM and usually don't leave until 4:00 or 5:00 PM. Following their grueling day at school, students who can afford it spend their evenings and weekends attending private classes, often until 10:00 PM or later. In these private classes, students receive extra training in the hopes of gaining a competitive edge in the examination process. It is not unusual for some students to spend 20 to 25 hours per week attending supplemental after-hours classes. The ultimate goal is to get accepted first into a so-called "good junior high school," then into a "good high school" and finally into a "good university."

With so many people and relatively few places available in China's universities, the entire education system is not so much geared to educating students as it is to weeding them out. Children are faced with hundreds of exams while going through primary and secondary school. Thrust into a fiercely competitive environment at an early age, the path to success is fraught with many obstacles and countless chances for failure. Only a select few who are lucky enough and clever enough manage to make it into a so-called "good university." This secures an almost guaranteed path to a decent career and a healthy financial future. The entire academic process, in effect, parallels the ancient Imperial examination system based on Confucian principles of learning.

The Chinese education system is not so much geared toward educating as toward weeding out students. Only the very brightest have any hope of succeeding.

The ideal Western classroom engenders participation, creativity through self-expression and development of one's imagination.

In the typical Chinese classroom teachers stress obedience, rote memorization and learning through repetition.

> *If you do not study hard when young,*
> *you'll end up bewailing your failures as you grow up.*
>
> **—Chinese proverb**

Corporal punishment is a regular facet of education in China. It is usually meted out for poor academic performance. Many parents agree with this practice.

MY DAY

7:00 Wash Class	4:00 Math Class
8:00 Assembly	5:00 get a snack
9:00 Math Test	5:30 English school
9:50 basketball	6:30 dinner/shower
10:00 Chinese Test	7:00 practice violin.
11:00 P.E.	8:00 Science school
12:00 lunch	9:00 Math school
12:50 sleep	10:00 study till 1:00
2:00 English Test	
3:00 Geography	Jimmy Wu

Throughout primary and secondary school, students undergo a rigorous schedule of study and examination. Those who can afford it also attend numerous after-hours classes to increase their competitive chances. For many students, 20 to 25 hours per week of supplemental classes is not unheard of.

Beginning in the first grade of elementary school, most students make their way to school between 6:30 and 7:00 AM. Students attending after-hours classes often study well past 9:00 or 10:00 PM. Bedtime for most elementary and junior high kids is 11:00 PM or later.

University Life

Unlike the typical Western education system, once accepted into a university, a Chinese student's life improves dramatically. Chinese people often say that childhood is a time to work hard but university life is a time to play. It is pretty much a reversal of standard Western views on childhood development.

In China, university students are secure in the knowledge that "they've made it." Getting expelled from university for any reason is virtually unheard of. Simply having achieved the impossible of actually surviving childhood and gaining entry into a post-secondary school is considered an adequate accomplishment in and of itself. University students spend a considerable amount of time joining various clubs and activities and essentially making up for their lost childhood.

One of the features of university training in China that strikes most Westerners as unusual is the widespread practice of plagiarism. Chinese students are products of a school system that tends to extinguish all forms of creative thought. Once in university, they are expected to write essays, term papers, presentations, etc.…and, lacking any experience in these skills, plagiarizing is the only way they can survive. Professors in China regularly hand out A's and B's for essays and papers which are blatantly lifted off the Internet or copied from a book. In Chinese universities, plagiarism is the norm rather than the exception.

At the university level in China, plagiarism is rampant.

In summary, the Chinese education system, founded on Confucian principles of learning, is a competitive system based on extensive testing. It stifles creative development and provides opportunities for only a tiny fraction of the total population. When interacting with people in China, keep in mind that almost all of them have suffered enormously under this system. It is best to cultivate a forgiving attitude toward those who sometimes seem unable to deal with situations requiring creative solutions—no matter how simple the problem may appear to you.

Confucian Influence #3: Focus on the Family

Unlike Western society, where individualism is encouraged and admired, Chinese society puts much more emphasis on the family as the primary unit of social organization. This stems from the Confucian idea of "filial piety." As a function of the Confucian hierarchy, filial piety was originally conceived as devotion and obedience one must show to one's parents—especially to one's father. Later, filial piety was extended to include one's ancestors. This gave rise to the practice of ancestor worship, which is ubiquitous in Chinese culture. In China, the family is everything—including those members who have passed into the great beyond.

Advantages

Having the family as the primary unit of society has a number of benefits in Chinese culture. First, Chinese families often live as extended families, with grandparents, uncles, aunts, etc. all living in close proximity to one another. Therefore, there is less need for government services designed to look after the elderly. In addition, grandparents often contribute greatly to the family unit. They usually take care of daily household tasks such as cooking and caring for the young. This allows both parents to take advantage of employment opportunities and to contribute to the family's financial well-being.

Second, focus on the family coupled with ancestor worship provides added impetus for "proper behavior" and conduct. In Chinese society, an individual's success belongs to the whole family. Conversely, an individual's shame also belongs to the entire family. If someone commits a crime, then he or she brings shame not only upon the entire family, but also on every single ancestor that came before. This provides a strong incentive for members of society to behave well.

Disadvantages

On the downside, heavy emphasis on the family unit has a few rather serious drawbacks. First, nepotism is a fundamental aspect of business and government in China. It pervades virtually every level of commerce and bureaucracy throughout the country. As such, many jobs are filled based on family ties and not on merit. The right person does not always necessarily end up in the right job. Furthermore, corruption, cronyism and mismanagement of funds are some of the major problems associated with nepotism in China's burgeoning business culture and bloated civil service. Nepotism is a powerful feature of Chinese society that seriously undermines any attempts at creating a system of governance based on merit and scholarship.

Another drawback of China's "family first" approach is that Chinese people tend to view society in terms of insiders and outsiders. Insiders consist of one's family, friends and associates. Outsiders are basically everyone else. Whereas loyalty to insiders is virtually unshakeable, feelings of responsibility to outsiders are often nonexistent.

Feelings of social and civic responsibility are by and large subservient to family loyalty and somewhat lacking in Chinese culture. Fortunately this tendency is countered by the Buddhist tenets of compassion and altruism. It must be noted of course that not everyone in China is a Buddhist. Long-term foreign residents living in China often complain that many Chinese people tend to be rather lacking in civic-minded behavior. Although undoubtedly a sweeping overgeneralization, it does highlight the disadvantage of perpetuating an "us" and "them" society.

By nature, men are nearly alike; by practice,
they get to be wide apart.

—Confucius

One outcome of Confucian notions on the family's supremacy in society is that Chinese people tend to view the world in terms of "us" and "them"—the insider/outsider phenomenon. A negative consequence of this phenomenon is that consideration for people outside one's inner circle sometimes appears nonexistent. The attitude "It doesn't affect my family, so why should I care?" often overrides feelings of civic responsibility and environmental concerns. Ultimately, it can lead to self-centered thinking and selfish behavior.

To see what is right and not to do it is want of courage.

—Confucius

As a dramatic example of how the insider/outsider worldview can have a negative impact on society, consider the following. In 2004 in Eastern China, an estimated 200 newborn babies starved to death. They died from consuming fake baby formula. The counterfeit baby food was found to contain one-sixth the amount of protein required to sustain life. It was distributed in packaging indistinguishable from a well-known name brand. Clearly, some individuals had an extreme lack of concern for what happens outside of their own personal group.

Vicious as a tigress can be, she never eats her own cubs.

—Chinese proverb

4

 RITUALS AND SUPERSTITIONS

During the Maoist era (1949–1976), religion was suppressed if not all but eradicated. Since the death of Mao Zedong in 1976, China has experienced a massive religious revival. With some exceptions (e.g., Falun Gong and some prohibited Christian sects), people are generally allowed to practice their religion freely and openly.

A fundamental aspect of religious devotion in China is the practice of spirit worship. This may take the form of worshipping one or more of the hundreds of Chinese deities. It also involves worshipping one's departed ancestors. Most spirit worship focuses on some kind of ritual. The most common ritual is burning incense offerings. Burning "ghost money" to provide a means of survival for one's dead ancestors is another popular ritual. Finally, people sometimes make food offerings to the dead.

In Chinese religious beliefs, the rules of ancestor worship dictate that offerings to the dead are the eldest son's responsibility. Without a son to perform the proper rites, a family's departed ancestors are unable to receive the proper offerings necessary for their survival in the afterlife. They are thus doomed for eternity to an existence of hunger and deprivation.

Parents without a male heir are of course themselves fated to eternal misery once they meet their inevitable demise. Once deceased, they too are condemned to wander for all eternity as "hungry ghosts." Having a son is therefore of paramount importance, especially for those people who take ancestor worship seriously.

In addition to engaging in ritualistic worship, many Chinese people are extremely superstitious. There are dozens, if not hundreds, of superstitions within Chinese culture. Rural Chinese tend to be more superstitious than their urban counterparts. The majority of educated urban Chinese tend to downplay the role of superstition in their lives. Even so, a lot of educated urbanites will still consult a fortuneteller before a major event like marriage or taking on a new job. It's always better to be safe than sorry.

Scores of factories devoted to producing religious statues and other religious items are sprouting up all over China. Religion is becoming big business.

Temples in China usually have a carnival-like atmosphere. People burn incense and other offerings to the Gods. They mill about with friends and family and generally relax in the pleasant atmosphere inside the ornately carved temples. There are usually snack shops and other facilities attached to the temple compound.

The four most popular things Chinese people pray for are: 1) Money and success; 2) Good health; 3) To have a son; and 4) Academic success.

As a function of their religious beliefs, Chinese people practice ancestor worship. Common rituals include setting up tables with beautifully decorated food offerings to dearly departed ones. Also, people often burn reams of "ghost money" in specially designed incineration bins. They believe that in doing so, their ancestors will be well provided for in the afterlife.

Those who know when they have enough are rich.

—Chinese proverb

Many Chinese consult a fortuneteller before major life events like marriage or having children. Popular fortunetelling techniques include astrology, palm reading, face reading and "Kau Cim," the practice of shaking a bamboo cylinder containing a number of modified incense sticks. These sticks are inscribed with Chinese characters. When a stick falls out of the cylinder, its characters are interpreted to formulate an answer to one's question.

A good fortune may forbode bad luck, which may in turn disguise a good fortune.

—Chinese proverb

FENG SHUI TIPS

GENTLY FLOWING WATER
CALMS THE MIND.

MOUNTAINS BACKING
YOUR HOUSE PROVIDE
POWERFUL SUPPORT
TO YOUR LIFE.

A CRYSTAL BALL PURIFIES AND
RAISES THE LEVEL OF CHI IN
YOUR ENVIRONMENT.

PLANT CHI ENCOURAGES
HEALING AND GROWTH IN
YOUR LIFE.

FISH ATTRACT PROSPERITY TO
YOUR HOME BY FLICKING AWAY
BAD LUCK WITH THEIR TAILS.

Feng shui, which translates as "Wind and Water," is the ancient Chinese art of achieving harmony with the environment. It focuses on life's vital energy (*chi*) and how it flows through our surroundings. Feng shui practitioners also attempt to explain how the environment, including our buildings, affects our health, finances and personal relationships.

Because when spoken in Chinese, the number four sounds very much like the word for "death," it is considered an unlucky number. Virtually all tall buildings have no fourth floor—just as many buildings in North America have no 13th floor.

Looking upon a corpse is considered risky business. There is a possibility that the dead person's ghost may haunt you.

In the 7th month of the Chinese lunar calendar (usually late July and early August), many Chinese people celebrate ghost month. It is widely believed that during this time, ghosts from the afterlife return to Earth to roam—very much like an extended version of Halloween. During this month, firecrackers explode at all hours of the day to chase ghosts away. In addition to this, people burn copious amounts of ghost money and make numerous food offerings in an effort to appease the spirits haunting the earthly plane. Traveling during ghost month is considered a dangerous affair. Some people believe that ghosts may cause accidents if they don't feel properly acknowledged.

Enjoy yourself. It's later than you think.

—Chinese proverb

A lot of Chinese people don't know how to swim. There is an inherent fear of water in Chinese culture. It is based on the belief that ghosts of drowning victims inhabit the seas. They are supposedly intent on having members of the living realm join them in their watery graves.

A common superstition is that counting steps while going up or down a staircase should be avoided. If you happen to make a mistake and miscount, you will disappear and your body will be sealed beneath the stairs for all eternity.

Another superstition is that hanging your clothing out to dry at night is dangerous. If you do so, ghosts will haunt your clothes.

If you have never done anything evil,
you should not be worrying about devils knocking at your door.

—Chinese proverb

5

"GUANXI" AND "MIANZI":

Two Concepts Crucial to Understanding Chinese People

Although there are a myriad of ways in which Western and Chinese cultures differ from one another, there are two fundamental aspects of Chinese society Westerners must understand in order to have successful interactions in China. They are the concepts of guanxi (pronounced "*guan-shee*") and mianzi (pronounced "*mee-enn-ze*").

Guanxi

The term *guanxi* is often translated into English as "connections" or "relationships." These terms, however, are insufficient to fully describe the importance of guanxi in Chinese life. Guanxi refers to the influence or "pull" that one can exert on one's social connections. It also refers to the social obligations a person has within one's network of contacts in society.

Sometimes Chinese people refer to their network of friends, contacts and associates (the "insiders" as discussed previously) as their guanxi circle. Perhaps though, it is more accurate to consider someone's guanxi circle as an intricate web. This web encompasses one's influence and personal obligations and it extends in an infinite number of directions within one's group.

In China, a person's guanxi network usually consists of the following: family, relatives, former classmates, coworkers, members of common clubs or organizations, former or present military cohorts as well as anyone else brought into the insider's circle. The relationships formed by these various associations are generally considered lifelong relationships—even if people lose touch with each other for years or even decades.

The relationships, which form one's inner circle, are nurtured primarily through the practice of reciprocating favors. It is a system of mutual obligation best summed up in the phrase "I scratch your back...you scratch mine." Returning favors is paramount to maintaining the web. Failure to reciprocate is tantamount to committing a major moral transgression.

Favors can be called in at any time: weeks, years or even decades after the granting of the initial favor. So if while in China, someone offers you a favor, it is important to realize the implications before accepting. Once you accept, you will essentially be locked into a never-ending cycle of giving and returning favors, a cycle lasting in perpetuity.

With the insider/outsider dichotomy permeating Chinese society, guanxi is fundamental to getting anything done in China. Guanxi is the grease that keeps the wheels turning. Perhaps nowhere else in the world does the phrase "It's all about who you know" have more relevance than it does in China. But it goes even deeper than that. It is not only about who you know. It is also about how the other person sees his or her obligations toward you. The more favors you do for someone, the more obligations they have toward you—and vice versa.

Anyone interested in doing business in China should begin cultivating guanxi as quickly as possible. When dealing with matters requiring government approval, people with the right connections can get around just about any official regulations with impunity. Also, China's vast bureaucracy is pretty much unnavigable without the right guanxi. It is critical if you ever hope to ensure that all the reams of applications get processed and all the right papers get rubber stamped in the right places.

One of the fastest ways to acquire guanxi is to hire relatives of a powerful local official. But be forewarned. As a foreigner, it may be assumed that you yourself have some pull with government officials in your own country. You may be expected to provide help with any number of problems beyond your actual scope of influence. These might include things like obtaining visas or perhaps letters of acceptance from prestigious universities for the children of your new Chinese connections. Failure to deliver on these expectations may result in your being labeled a "bad friend." This could seriously restrict your influence within the guanxi web. You may even find yourself excluded from your network altogether and have to start the process of cultivating guanxi all over again.

○ BROTHER
△ SISTER
□ CLASSMATE
✳ MILITARY FRIEND
◉ SISTER'S HUSBAND
◇ FATHER'S FRIEND
MOTHER'S FRIEND
● CLASSMATE'S BROTHER
▲ CLASSMATE'S FRIEND
■ FATHER'S COUSIN
✷ COUSIN'S COUSIN
◆ COUSIN'S FRIEND
◖ UNCLE'S CLASSMATE
☾ AUNT'S FRIEND
◗ CLASSMATE'S FATHER
⊕ MOTHER'S CLASSMATE
◉ CLASSMATE'S COUSIN
◆ BROTHER'S CLASSMATE
◓ CLASSMATE'S AUNT

Guanxi refers to one's network of connections and associates. Moreover, it refers to one's influence on those connections as well as to one's obligations toward members of the group. Maintenance of relationships within the network is accomplished primarily through acts of reciprocating favors.

> *When drinking water from a well, one should never forget who dug it.*
>
> **—Chinese proverb**

One's obligations toward others in one's guanxi web are best summed up with the phrase "I scratch your back…you scratch mine." In China, failure to reciprocate on a favor within one's guanxi web is no mere faux pas; it is almost considered a mortal sin.

The most common method of sustaining one's network of contacts is by going out for a meal or a banquet—preferably at an expensive restaurant. If you are a guest at a banquet, be forewarned. Most banquet style meals consist of anywhere from 10 to 14 courses. So pace yourself. Don't eat too much during the first few courses. Be sure to leave enough room to sample a bit of everything. Failure to do so may insult your host by leaving the impression that you don't like the food and don't appreciate their generosity.

Everyone eats and drinks; yet only few appreciate the taste of food.

—Confucius

Guanxi is the oil that keeps the wheels turning in Chinese society. Without guanxi, it is pretty much impossible to accomplish anything in China.

Mianzi: Face

Confucius taught that if you lead people "with excellence and put them in their place through roles and ritual practices, in addition to developing a sense of shame, they will order themselves harmoniously" (Analects II, 3). Largely as a result of Confucian teachings, China has evolved into a shame-based culture. This is very different from Western, conscience-based cultures founded on traditional Christian teachings. In effect, people in China "behave properly" generally because they want to avoid shame and they fear losing face—not necessarily because they might feel badly about their actions. For a lot of Chinese people, anything goes—as long as you don't get caught.

Of all the idiosyncrasies found in Chinese culture, perhaps the most difficult for Westerners to comprehend and fully appreciate is the concept of mianzi or "face." The closest terms for mianzi in English are "dignity" or "prestige." These terms, however, do not fully encapsulate the concept. "Face" also refers to the pride one feels in one's self-concept coupled with the way one is viewed by others.

Unlike in Western culture where you either have dignity or you don't, in China, "face" can be given or earned. It can also be taken away or lost. To many Westerners, Chinese people often appear to be obsessed with issues of face. Also, most Westerners tend to underestimate the important role face plays as a key motivator governing Chinese behavior.

So what exactly is face all about? Essentially, anything that raises someone's self esteem results in gaining face whereas anything that lowers one's esteem in the eyes of others results in a loss of face. Causing someone to gain face is a good thing, however, causing someone to lose face can have very serious ramifications.

If you've ever had the opportunity to live in China and if at any time you've inexplicably lost a friend, a contract or a customer, chances are you did something to cause someone to lose face. Unfortunately, there are many ways you can cause someone to lose face. Behaviors such as interrupting someone, declining an invitation to dinner or perhaps not showing the proper deference to one's superiors can all lead to face-losing situations. In a Western context, these kinds of behaviors are usually considered to be innocuous slights that are overlooked and quickly forgotten. But in Chinese society, these seemingly minor indiscretions can sometimes insult someone so deeply as to create an enemy for life!

Because of the face issue, Westerners are often quick to label their Chinese counterparts as touchy or hypersensitive; but note, that is the Western point of view. When in China, your best policy is to avoid causing anyone to lose face. Causing someone to lose face is very serious business. If you make someone lose face, you may encounter some unpleasant repercussions. For example, if you happen to cause an employee to publicly lose face, he or she will likely seek revenge through some form of sabotage or non-compliant behavior. Also, if you happen to cause a government official to lose face, then be prepared to wait indefinitely for any application approvals from his or her office. Chances are, you will be waiting for a very long time, probably forever.

Chinese people often go to great lengths to avoid a loss of face. If possible, when interacting with Chinese people, always leave them a way out of any face-losing situation. If you stay in China long enough, you will probably find that in contests between face and the truth, face wins out every time. In Chinese culture, it is perfectly acceptable to tell a lie, even a bald-faced lie, if it serves to preserve face. If you ever catch someone in the act of lying to preserve face, go along with it and don't back them into a corner. If you choose to call them on it, you will no doubt be considered a very rude and perhaps even a very cruel person. You will also need to prepare yourself for any possible future acts of revenge. As mentioned earlier, face is a very serious matter in China. It's best not to treat it lightly.

Do good, reap good; do evil, reap evil.

—Chinese proverb

The Top 12 Ways of Giving or Gaining Face

Giving someone a sincere compliment.

Praising someone publicly.

Obviously enjoying oneself when being treated by one's Chinese associates.

Treating someone to an expensive meal or a banquet.

Obviously going out of one's way to do something for someone.

Receiving an expensive gift, especially an imported one.

Being rich. Chinese people love money. They don't share the same uneasiness many Westerners feel when talking about money or making financial transactions. The idea of money as "filthy lucre" is completely absent in Chinese society. Getting rich truly is considered to be glorious.

Being lucky. Throughout Asia, gambling is a popular pastime.

Earning a college degree from a prestigious university.

Marrying well.

Having a son.

Having a successful child.

The Top 12 Ways of Losing Face or Making Someone Else Lose Face

Not showing proper deference to one's elders or superiors.

Criticizing someone publicly.

Turning down an invitation with an outright "No." In China, saying "No" to a request is considered rude or impolite. The most common ways of saying "No" in China are: 1) Maybe; 2) Yes, maybe; and 3) I will discuss it with so and so.

Being late on a flimsy excuse.

Interrupting someone while they are talking.

Threatening to fire someone or actually firing them.

Catching someone in a lie and exposing it. Telling lies is a common way of preserving face in Chinese culture.

Becoming angry with someone. Showing anger often results in a mutual loss of face for both parties involved.

Not being able to do something—especially not being able to speak English. Many Chinese go out of their way to avoid interacting with Westerners. This is because they are embarrassed about their inability to speak English. (FYI: To fully appreciate the humor in the illustration above, please note that the common name for Viagra in China is "Mighty Brother.")

Admitting to having made a mistake is a rather serious loss of face. Try your best to avoid forcing anyone into doing this. Always leave them a way out even if it means accepting a bald-faced lie.

Admitting to not knowing something can also result in a serious loss of face. Often, misleading information is given as a means of preserving face.

Getting "fall down drunk" can result in a loss of face. The ability to hold one's liquor is generally seen as a sign of stamina and strength. It's a macho thing.

6

CULTURE SHOCK

The term "culture shock" refers to a complex set of emotions one experiences when exposed to an alien environment. When first arriving in a strange country, everything looks and feels different. The local geography, climate, flora and fauna, urban environment and even the way people look are some of the first things travelers notice when disembarking in their destination country.

During the first few days in a foreign environment, people often experience feelings of excitement, elation, anticipation and a sense of wonder. As time goes by, however, it's not uncommon for these initial feelings of excitement to be replaced with feelings of anxiety, disorientation, bewilderment and often frustration. The stress associated with living in a foreign environment begins to take its toll.

Often the main contributor to travel-related stress is the language barrier. Unless one has studied one's destination country's language in advance, no matter how intelligent or educated one may be, landing in a foreign country automatically renders you functionally illiterate. All the signs and billboards are in a foreign language. Radio and TV broadcasts are also predominantly indecipherable. Even the chatter one hears in everyday conversation sounds alien and strange.

As a functional illiterate in a strange land, one finds that simple everyday tasks like finding an address or ordering a meal can sometimes turn into a major production. It often requires enlisting the help of any number of people. These are usually sympathetic strangers who, more often than not, converse with you in their native tongue. It's enough to make even the brightest of people feel helpless and somewhat dim-witted at times. Unfortunately, in many cases, inhabitants of your host country may view you in this same light. For some people, it can be quite humiliating and degrading.

Most social scientists would say that culture shock tends to progress through three distinct phases: 1) the Honeymoon Phase; 2) the Frustration Phase; and 3) the Acceptance and Resignation Phase. It is important to note that if your duration of stay in a foreign country lasts for an extended period of time, it is possible to randomly move in and out of all three phases in a nonlinear fashion at any given time.

The Honeymoon Phase

The honeymoon phase of culture shock is the most pleasant of all phases. It normally occurs at the beginning of a journey into a foreign environment. During this phase, everything is wonderful. The strange and new environment is exciting and highly stimulating. The happy traveler has the opportunity to experience many amazing new things, often for the first time. New discoveries typically include exotic foods and beverages, unusual sights and sounds, the exciting hustle and bustle in the cities or perhaps some stunning natural beauty in the countryside. During the honeymoon phase, even commercials on TV can be an endless source of enjoyment and wonder. It's very much like falling in love.

To know the road ahead, ask those coming back.

—Chinese proverb

Phase 1: The Honeymoon Phase. Everything is beautiful and stimulating and oh so wonderful!

The Frustration Phase

In phase two of culture shock, the honeymoon is over. After weeks or months of being a stranger in a strange land, the simple act of survival begins to feel tedious and sometimes overwhelming. Most menus in restaurants are unreadable and all the strange and exotic foods discovered in the first few weeks of your travels start to lose their appeal. Not knowing your way around and getting lost all the time is no longer any fun. The countless hours spent seeking out common Western goods, such as peanut butter and jam, begin to feel like so much wasted time. To make matters worse, the almost daily ritual of being treated like an imbecile by shopkeepers and bus drivers because you can't speak the local language causes frustration levels to rise. Sooner or later it's inevitable… you snap! A sudden, explosive tirade launched at a perfect stranger on the street is a definite sign that you've made it into phase two of culture shock. It's usually during this phase that most foreigners pack their bags and go home.

Phase 2: The Frustration Phase. This is the phase in which Westerners invariably find a way to perpetuate their reputation in China as "Foreign Devils."

The Acceptance and Resignation Phase

In the final phase of culture shock, a feeling of calm resignation takes over. Everyday life becomes rather normal. The daily hassles of survival no longer seem so frustrating and unbearable. Don't be complacent though. Phases one or two of culture shock can always unexpectedly creep back into your consciousness. Just when you think you've seen it all, a pleasant experience can trigger feelings of being in love all over again with your host country. Equally so, a negative encounter with a stranger or perhaps a cultural misunderstanding with a friend may trigger feelings of frustration and anger completely out of proportion to the situation. Stay calm. Be patient. Everything works out eventually.

Phase 3: The Acceptance and Resignation Phase. Everything is okay. Life is okay. It may not be fantastic but it's all good.

Overcoming Culture Shock

One of the best ways to overcome the negative aspects of culture shock is to immerse yourself in your new culture and avail yourself of all it has to offer. Too often, Westerners living in a foreign culture stick to their small group of expatriate friends and isolate themselves from their host country. Gatherings of these groups very often deteriorate into "expat bitch sessions." These little get-togethers usually involve people sitting around, drinking beer and complaining about all the problems related to being a visible minority in a strange land. This behavior tends to perpetuate all the negative emotions related to culture shock.

The expat bitch session.

In China, there are many interesting activities to engage in to alleviate the negative feelings associated with living in a foreign land. For fitness and health, you can try learning tai chi or kung fu. If you have an artistic bent, you can try taking a class in Chinese pottery or Chinese calligraphy. Because China has one of the most diverse forms of cuisine in the world, taking a class in Chinese cooking is a great way to increase your culinary repertoire. Learning about the local culture by visiting a museum or exploring your immediate environs can broaden your perspective on your host country. Best of all, studying Chinese can help you overcome the language barrier and allow you to form meaningful and fulfilling relationships with the locals. All of these methods are excellent ways to make new friends and appreciate the many positive aspects of living in a foreign country.

7
GENERAL PECULIARITIES

When in China, you will undoubtedly notice many differences between China and your home country. You will certainly discover differences in climate, differences in architecture, differences in behavior and differences in the way things are done. Also, Chinese society offers several cultural peculiarities that most Westerners may find somewhat odd. These idiosyncrasies tend to vary from region to region.

In the big cities, people generally tend to have had more contact with foreigners. As such, many people in these areas are somewhat westernized and less likely to display traditional values and behaviors. Also, they are less likely to see you as a curiosity worthy of close scrutiny.

As you move away from the big urban centers and go into the countryside, cultural differences become more pronounced. People in these regions tend to be more traditional in their outlook. As outsiders, foreigners attract a fair amount of attention. This is usually in the form of staring, pointing, attempts at conversation, and most commonly, in the form of endless choruses of "Hellos" shouted at you from all directions. Very often, it feels much like being a celebrity rock star of sorts.

The following illustrations highlight some general aspects of China and Chinese culture that sometimes strike Westerners as strange or unusual. If you stay in China for only a short time, you will probably not encounter all of these peculiarities. If, however, you stay for an extended period of time, you will likely have a chance to experience them all.

In many parts of China, winters are brutally cold.

In many parts of China, summers are extremely hot.

Architecture in China seems to be mostly from the school of "Drab and Ugly."

The media in China is tightly controlled. Many news stories consist primarily of jingoistic propaganda geared toward stirring up fervent patriotic national pride.

Access to information on the Internet is highly controlled. Gaining entry to many foreign websites is spotty at best. The situation is pretty much in a constant state of flux. On many sites, access is sometimes denied, then granted, and then later denied again.

China's infrastructure is still in a state of development throughout much of the country. Power cuts are frequent in many places. It's not all bad though. There are many pleasant activities one can engage in during recurrent blackouts—playing cards, sing-alongs, etc....

ASIAN RESTROOM

Restrooms in China fall into two general categories: 1) Western style throne commodes and 2) Asian style squatter commodes. Sometimes there is a third variation, a hybrid throne commode with foot grips on the seat cover for squatting, but this is rare. In China, squatters generally outnumber thrones 10 to 1. Getting used to squatters takes a little practice and some Westerners never really seem to get the hang of it.

Furthermore, drainage pipes in restroom facilities are designed with narrow gauge pipes. These cannot accommodate paper so there is always a trash can in washroom facilities for used toilet paper. Don't forget to use the trash can, unless you fancy the notion of eventually being on a first name basis with your local plumber. Also, if you happen to have Western style facilities in your home, don't be surprised to find footprints on the seat cover after having company over. Many people in China are not all too clear on the concept of the throne commode.

First Impressions

During initial encounters in China, there is a strong likelihood you may be asked personal questions that are considered rude and intrusive in Western culture. Try to maintain a sense of humor and realize that these questions are not intended to be offensive. They are sincere attempts at reaching out and trying to establish a sense of closeness leading to a positive interaction.

Chinese people say their family name first when giving their names. Married women keep their family names after marriage. Children take their father's family name. It is a patrilineal society. Unless directed otherwise, the appropriate designation to use when addressing a married woman is "Miss," followed by her family name. For men, "Mister" followed by his family name is also fine. Ideally though, when applicable, using a person's professional title is definitely the best option, for example, "Professor Chang" or "Director Lee."

Words are the voice of the heart.

—Confucius

Don't forget, we all look the same to them. Many Chinese are sometimes under the impression that foreigners all somehow know each other.

Upon meeting people in China, the standard handshake generally falls into the category of limp fish. Try not to squeeze too hard. You might freak someone out.

Issues of Personal Space

The Chinese concept of personal space is very different from the Western notion. In face-to-face communication, the average North American requires a minimum of 45 cm (approximately 18 inches) of distance from the other person. In China, it's much closer, 25–30 cm (approximately 10–12 inches). This difference in personal space is often a source of great discomfort for many Westerners. It takes a little getting used to. A good supply of breath mints and a healthy sense of humor are usually all that is required.

A smile will gain you ten more years of life.

—Chinese proverb

Maintaining North American standards of personal space in a lineup will invariably result in people assuming that you are not actually waiting in line. They will most certainly cut in front of you with not so much as an "excuse me."

When shopping in a supermarket, don't be surprised if entire families take great interest in the contents of your shopping cart. Lots of smiling and pointing is inevitably part of the exchange but it's all in good fun. Many Chinese people are not used to seeing foreigners, especially in the countryside. They're just curious, that's all.

If banking in China, try not to be alarmed when someone looks over your shoulder to peer at your bankbook or withdrawal slip while you are at the teller. Don't worry. It's harmless. It's only an expression of genuine curiosity and nothing more.

Most people in China sport jet-black hair and Chinese men generally don't have all that much body or facial hair. The Western barbarian look for men and the fair-haired look for Western women are sources of great curiosity and fascination for many Chinese people—especially children. Chinese children often instinctively try to obtain hair samples for analysis.

Some Common Interactions

Chinese people frequently comment on your physical appearance. Many Westerners who travel to China are delighted to suddenly discover that they are very handsome or very beautiful.

Good words are like a string of pearls.

—Chinese proverb

If you happen to be a little bit overweight, expect to hear about it sooner or later. If you are more than a little overweight, you will probably hear about it much more often. Sometimes it will be directly to your face or sometimes it will be behind your back in Chinese. Hopefully you're not an oversensitive type.

It's not unusual to have Chinese people pointing and obviously talking about you. It can make you feel a little paranoid at times. Usually though, they are not saying anything bad. In the example above, the two Chinese girls are laughing at their friend who is thinking about going over and attempting to converse in English with the foreign girl.

Out in public, people often come up to you and engage in conversation. They often state openly that they would like to practice their English with you. It's up to you to decide whether or not to play along. Some foreigners enjoy it while others despise having their personal space invaded upon. Feel free to feign unconsciousness or an inability to speak English if you don't feel like giving out free language lessons.

A single conversation with a wise man is better than ten years of study.

—Chinese proverb

Standards of Beauty: Male/Female Relationships

The Western standard of male good looks (e.g., a prominent chin and a big muscular body) is not necessarily considered attractive to the average Chinese woman. Add excessive facial and body hair into the mix and the turnoff is pretty much complete.

Judging by images found in popular culture, it appears that the ideal standard of good looks for men in China includes wavy hair, a slight build and cute, youthful and slightly effeminate features.

Western standards of female beauty (e.g., taller than average and curvaceous) may serve more to intimidate than to attract Chinese men. To make matters worse, the only exposure most Chinese males have to foreign females is through watching movies. It is quite common for Western women to feel stereotyped while in China. (FYI: "Blue movies" are called "yellow movies" in China.)

Based on images provided in Chinese movies and TV, it seems the ideal standard of beauty for women in China includes fair skin, a petite figure and cute, youthful features.

In China, public displays of affection between members of the same sex are pretty much the norm. Men walking arm in arm and women holding hands are things you see practically every day. And no, it doesn't necessarily mean someone is gay. It's just what people do.

When choosing a mate, the Chinese usually base their decision on practical concerns rather than on looks. As such, a lot of Chinese women actively seek out foreign men as potential mates—regardless of their physical appearance. This is done based on the perception that all foreigners are rich. Chinese men, however, generally stay away from Western women. This is mostly because Western women, by and large, don't measure up to Chinese ideals of femininity that generally include a meek, obedient demeanor. Sorry girls.

If you are male and decide to get a haircut in China, be wary of the fact that a significant number of barbershops operate as fronts for brothels—often run by the local police force. If you aren't careful, you may end up with a very expensive bad haircut and perhaps a little bit more pampering than you bargained for.

Get rid of cleverness and abandon profit,
and thieves and gangsters will not exist.

—Lao Tzu

While in China you may encounter a rather interesting phenomenon. Sometimes attractive Chinese women deliberately seek out mates who are significantly less attractive than they are. The main reason is that a so-called "ugly husband" is less likely to be unfaithful. Women who go this route are usually quite proud of their choice, especially if the husband is a good earner.

In Chinese families, women generally hold the purse strings and manage the family's financial affairs.

Attitudes on Race

A well-known joke in China involves a creation myth with God as a baker. When God made humans, he first made black people and they were overcooked. Next he made white people and they were undercooked. Finally, he made Chinese people and they were just perfect. This little story reflects quite well the Chinese sense of racial superiority relative to the rest of the world.

Despite what most Chinese people may tell you regarding racism against dark-skinned people in China (i.e. "It doesn't exist"), the opposite is true. It is partially a result of negative stereotypes propagated by Western media. It also stems from an inherent cultural bias against having dark skin. This bias is based on a common perception that equates skin color with social rank. If your skin happens to be of the non-pink variety, you may face negative consequences while in China. For example, you may encounter excessive staring and pointing. You may also miss out on potential job opportunities. Unfortunately, in China, racism against dark-skinned people is a sad fact of life.

There is a double standard in the way different foreigners are treated in China. Generally, foreigners from developed "rich" countries are treated with more consideration and respect than foreigners from less developed "poor" countries.

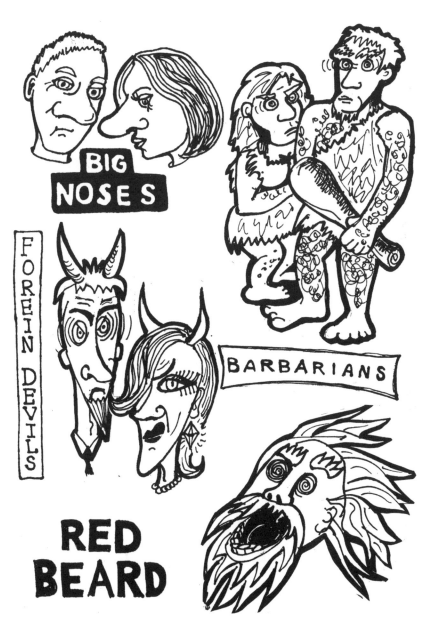

BIG NOSES

FOREIN DEVILS

BARBARIANS

RED BEARD

While generally welcoming toward Westerners, many Chinese still view foreigners with a certain amount of derision. Some common nicknames for foreigners in China include the following: 1) Foreign Devil; 2) Barbarian; 3) Big Nose; and 4) Red Beard. These terms frequently pop up in newspapers and other media when topics include some form of discussion regarding Westerners.

OUT AND ABOUT:
ENCOUNTERING THE PECULIAR

The following illustrations focus on specific facets of Chinese society you might encounter while in China. For many Westerners, adjusting to certain aspects of Chinese culture can be quite trying at times. One of the keys to a happy life in China lies in a willingness to learn about and accept the many cultural differences between East and West. Of course, it always helps to maintain a good sense of humor.

Communication

Chinese is one of the most difficult languages to learn. It is a tonal language. This means that word syllables, which sound identical to the Western ear, take on radically different meanings depending on the inflection used. In some ways it resembles music.

Imagine for a moment that while speaking English, the words "she," "she," "she" and "she" could all take on radically different meanings—depending on which musical notes were used and how they were "sung" while speaking. Depending on the tone used for each word, the first one might mean "snake," the second one might mean "ten," the third one might mean "is" and the fourth one might mean "what?" Hopefully this gives you a general idea of the difficulties associated with the Chinese language. Moreover, the difficulties in learning to read and write Chinese surpass anything you will face in learning to speak it. If learning Chinese is one of your goals in life, I wish you good luck!

When trying to communicate in Chinese, if you lack a proper appreciation for the subtleties of the language, you will not likely be understood. Furthermore, you may be laughed at, ridiculed or looked down upon for not being able to do something any three-year-old can do with ease. Don't let it get you down and keep trying. Most Chinese people are quite forgiving and will sincerely appreciate your efforts.

If a Chinese person ever says that you speak Chinese well, don't believe it. Unless you are in actual fact truly adept in Chinese, praise for your linguistic prowess is most definitely a sincere attempt to alleviate your embarrassment and help you to preserve face. In the illustration above, the Westerner is trying to say, "Hello. Nice to meet you. I like Chinese people. We are friends." Owing to the improper use of tonal inflections, he is actually saying, "You vast. Fertile hate shine apricot people are mud. Fertile giggle bracelet loyal monkey people. Fertile door vast bump oil." Small wonder Chinese people sometimes think Westerners are not all that bright.

If you understand others you are smart.
If you understand yourself you are illuminated.

—Lao Tzu

When ordering plane, train or bus tickets while in China, it is best to get a Chinese friend to help you. Even the slightest mispronunciation could result in you being sent to the opposite end of the country.

If you ever have the opportunity to witness Chinese group decision-making, it may strike you as rather odd. In groups, Westerners typically make quick decisions based on a snap vote. In China, groups tend to discuss and discuss and discuss some more. Trying to establish a consensus that is acceptable to everyone is part of the Confucian focus on maintaining social harmony.

In everyday conversation, Westerners always answer a negatively phrased question with a negative response. For example:

Question: "So you haven't eaten dinner yet?"

Answer: "No."

In China, the answer to this question would be "Yes"—meaning, "Yes, you're right, I haven't eaten dinner yet." Admittedly, the typical Chinese response is more logical than the Western response. This very simple difference in logical approach, however, can lead to miscommunication with potentially disastrous consequences. Avoid using negatively phrased questions when talking to people in China. Instead, use direct questions that can be answered clearly with "Yes" or "No."

When a Chinese person does something wrong, they usually laugh or giggle. For Westerners this can be infuriating. Not only did someone just cause some kind of distress, but now they think it's funny! This of course is not the case. The laughter is in fact nervous laughter and it is very much a reflex response designed to hopefully defuse the situation and try to preserve face. Don't let it get to you when it happens.

The hand gesture for beckoning someone in China resembles a waving motion with the palm of the hand facing down. Don't be surprised if you have people running toward you every time you wave goodbye.

One of the things you may notice in China is the strange phenomenon of "Chinglish." Many factories in China do not have any native English speakers on their staff. Oddly enough, a lot of these factories mass-produce T-shirts, billboards, product labels and even scooters peppered with nonsense English slogans. It's not all that different from Westerners sporting Chinese character tattoos that say "Ger" or "De" just because they look hip.

If you know, recognize that you know. If you don't know,
then realize that you don't know. That is knowledge.

—Confucius

Being a Celebrity

While out and about in China, Western foreigners are often granted near celebrity status. When sightseeing in tourist spots, it's quite normal for perfect strangers to ask if you would like to pose for a picture with them.

Foreigners who make an effort to adopt local customs, such as eating with chopsticks, are often a source of great fascination for Chinese people. The simple fact that you're trying to adopt local ways very often raises your esteem in the eyes of your Chinese hosts disproportionately to the actual effort involved.

If you ever happen to get lost in China, you may be pleasantly surprised. Many Chinese are sympathetic and extremely helpful toward foreigners who have lost their way. They genuinely feel sorry for lone travelers. Most Chinese people travel in large groups. The idea of being all alone in a foreign country is considered by many to be a frightening concept.

Well-endowed Western women may face unwanted attention in the form of pointing and laughing. It can be very annoying.

One of the interesting features of China's social landscape is the long-term foreign resident who is very often a local celebrity of sorts. This person is usually a Western male married to a local female. These "lifers" are by and large invaluable sources of information and guidance. They are normally more than happy to share information and experiences. Sometimes they seem somewhat starved for the company of their compatriots.

It is often apparent that long-term residency has caused lifers to "go native"—that is to say, they've adopted local cultural attitudes and values. For some reason, however, these "new Chinese" are sometimes rather critical of their adopted culture. Perhaps it's a negative consequence of feeling isolated in a foreign land.

Visiting and Dining

When visiting Chinese people in their homes, you must take off your shoes. Usually, you will be provided with a pair of slippers or flip-flops that are often many sizes too small. If no slippers are provided, socks or bare feet are both perfectly acceptable.

Chinese people can be some of the most hospitable people you will ever encounter.

When dining out, Chinese people love a raucous, noisy environment. Loud talking, endless toasting, clanging dishes and the general hustle and bustle all contribute to the overall enjoyment of the meal. The word they use to describe this type of environment is *re nau*. It means "hot and raucous." It is very much a celebration of life and can truly be an enjoyable experience.

At the end of a meal in a restaurant, don't be alarmed if several members of your dinner party suddenly make a run for the cashier and jockey for the right to pay for the entire bill. It's all part of the entertaining process and is rooted in Confucian teachings on the value of hospitality and generosity. It's also a great way for the one paying the bill to gain face by demonstrating a benevolent nature. If you are the one being treated, sit back and watch the fun. If you happen to be the host of the dinner party, arrange for advance payment with the restaurant staff to avoid others stealing your glory as a generous host.

To be able under all circumstances to practice five things constitutes perfect virtue; these five things are gravity, generosity of soul, sincerity, earnestness and kindness.

—Confucius

Shopping

Compared to the 1970s, when cheating foreigners was an official government-sanctioned practice, the situation regarding this problem is much improved. With more and more shops adopting fixed sticker prices on their goods, the likelihood of getting ripped off is much less these days than before. Nevertheless, in situations requiring haggling, in order to avoid getting fleeced, it pays to shop around. It's also wise to ask a Chinese friend about the going rate on the products you're considering buying.

> *Possessing rare treasures brings about harmful behavior.*
>
> *—Lao Tzu*

If you happen to be taller or bigger than average, it may be somewhat difficult to find clothing that fits properly.

For Western women, shopping for underwear can be a bit of a hassle. It's not always easy to find the right size.

While out shopping or maybe while watching TV, you may notice an amazing number of pharmaceutical products targeted at female consumers. These medicines and potions are usually designed for skin whitening, losing weight or for breast augmentation. Most of them don't work.

Despite government attempts at cracking down on counterfeit goods, the concept of intellectual property rights is almost nonexistent in China. Estimates suggest that 80 to 90% of all software, music and movie DVDs are pirated. Cheap movies sold on the streets are popular with foreign expatriates living in China and are generally seen as one of the perks of living in the Wild East.

The pirating of electronic goods is a growing trend in China. The more sophisticated counterfeiters not only put a famous brand name on a fake product but they even go to the extreme of building fake stores. These come complete with signs, display cases and staff uniforms, which are identical to those of the company whose goods they are copying. So next time you're in a Sony store in China, you may end up paying top dollar for what is in fact not a true Sony product but actually a "Bony" TV or a "Baloney" DVD player—all displaying of course the Sony label and indistinguishable from the real thing.

Never seek illicit wealth.

—*Confucius*

Naturally, the clothing and fashion industry is also prone to rampant counterfeiting. Fake brand names are literally everywhere and very easy to come by.

A growing problem in China and throughout much of Asia is the issue of counterfeit medicine. A grave threat to public health, fake drugs now account for up to 25% of the total prescription drug market. Usually fake drugs contain harmless substances but all too often, they are made with toxic materials that lead to sickness and even death for the hapless consumer.

Health and Medicine

Much to the delight of the tobacco industry, smoking is a popular vice in China—primarily among men.

Upon first meeting someone, there is a good chance you will be offered a cigarette. It's okay to decline the offer.

If you wake up very early in the morning and go to a park, you will undoubtedly see a number of people practicing Tai Chi or some other kind of fitness regimen. According to Traditional Chinese Medicine (TCM), in the early hours of the day, trees emit a great amount of *chi*, the mystical life force that animates the entire universe. By doing exercise in close proximity to trees early in the morning, one can absorb the excess *chi*. It is reckoned to be very good for one's health.

Basketball is gaining popularity as a pastime in China. In an interesting leap of logic, a lot of Chinese people sincerely believe that playing basketball can help make you taller. The logic goes like this: Basketball players are tall. All basketball players play basketball. Therefore playing basketball obviously makes you tall.

In summer, if you go out to a park or somewhere in nature, you will probably see men with their shirts pulled up and their bellies exposed. They are aerating their navels in order to cool down and improve their overall health by absorbing *chi* through their exposed bellies.

Spitting to clean out one's sinuses is considered a natural body function beneficial to one's health and is very common in China. It is usually preceded by a loud, grating throat-clearing sound.

Traditional Chinese Medicine: TCM

Health care in China is divided into two major categories: Western medicine and Traditional Chinese Medicine (TCM). Chinese people generally consult Western style doctors for acute or life-threatening conditions. Traditional Chinese doctors are usually consulted for chronic and less serious conditions. Much of TCM is rooted in Taoist philosophy. TCM practitioners generally have a holistic approach to healing. The focus is on prevention and on maintaining balance and harmony throughout the various systems in the human body.

The most popular forms of Chinese medicine are Acupuncture, Reflexology, Cupping, Herbal medicine and Chi Gong healing.

1. Acupuncture: The practice of inserting needles at specified points in the body. This is done to free up blockages in one's chi and to establish a balanced state in the human body.
2. Reflexology: A form of treatment that uses massage to remove blockages in one's chi and establish proper flow.

3. Cupping: The practice of placing suction cups on specified parts of the body to accomplish pretty much the same goal as acupuncture and reflexology.
4. Herbal medicine: The treatment of illness using the medicinal properties of a wide range of plants and herbs. The goal is to establish and maintain balance throughout the various systems in the body.
5. Chi Gong Healing: A Chi Gong healer uses non-contact treatment to manipulate a patient's chi and bring it into balance.

One of the criticisms leveled at Traditional Chinese Medicine by Western environmentalists is the use of animal parts from endangered species. Indeed, TCM's use of threatened and declining species is a major conservation issue. Some endangered animals whose parts are used in TCM include rhinos, tigers, leopards and turtles. Contrary to popular misconceptions about TCM, parts from these animals are not used as aphrodisiacs to treat sexual dysfunction. Rather, they are used mostly as anti-inflammatory tonics to treat medical conditions such as arthritis and inflammation.

Another controversial aspect of TCM that tends to outrage animal lovers is the practice of using bear bile as a treatment for various illnesses. These ailments include asthma, cancer and liver complaints. Currently, there are an estimated 9,000 captive bears in China and another 4,000 in Vietnam. These bears are kept for their entire lives in steel cages not much larger than their bodies. Bile is extracted through a process known as "milking": an incision is made in the abdomen and a tube is inserted permanently into the gall bladder from which bile drips down into a pan on the floor.

Once the bears are too old to produce sufficient quantities of bile, they are normally left to starve or they are killed outright. Their gall bladders are then removed and used for medicinal purposes. Furthermore, their paws are cut off and sold to restaurants for human consumption. Bear claws are considered a tasty delicacy.

Animal rights activists also take great exception to many practices regarding the ethical treatment of cats and dogs in China. Dog meat, though very expensive in China, is eaten as a health tonic in many parts of the country. Often these animals are boiled or skinned alive because torture is believed to enhance

To cure disease is like waiting until one is thirsty
before digging a well.

—Li Shizhen, 16th-century physician

the flavor of the meat. In addition, over 2 million cats and dogs are slaughtered annually for their fur, which is sold in North America and Europe. There, it is used in the manufacture of gloves, toys for pets and trim for coats.

Although the mistreatment of animals occurs in some parts of China, it must be noted that many Chinese as well as many TCM practitioners condemn such

activities. It is not fair to paint the entire country as a bastion of brutality because of the actions and attitudes of a minority of Chinese people. With Buddhism as a major influence in Chinese culture, the majority of Chinese people do not condone animal cruelty. Nonetheless, it is still a rather significant problem that demands a solution.

If ever faced with the prospect of consuming animal parts from an endangered species, it is best to refuse. You can offer the excuse that your Chinese doctor recommends you stick to herbal remedies for your health and well-being.

Much to the horror and dismay of Western dog lovers, many Chinese pet owners keep their dogs in steel cages and seldom or never take them out for a walk.

While condemning Chinese society for its mistreatment of animals, it is also important to examine our own practices of animal cruelty. For example, the Western practice of starving young calves in cramped conditions in order to produce lean veal is widely considered cruel and inhumane. So is the practice in France of force-feeding geese to produce oversized livers for the production of pâté de foie gras. Most cultures are guilty of animal mistreatment in some form or other.

Be not afraid of growing slowly, be afraid only of standing still.

—Chinese proverb

9

TRANSPORTATION ISSUES

China is currently undergoing an unprecedented explosive boom in its car industry. In 2007, China had an estimated 12 million cars on the road. By the year 2020, that number is expected to rise to 120 million. Road construction is unable to keep pace with China's car revolution. Already, in cities like Beijing and Shanghai, brand new freeways look like six-lane parking lots during rush hour.

China's Thirst for Oil

Moreover, China's thirst for oil is growing at an exponential rate. In 1994, China was completely self-sufficient in terms of its energy needs. Today, China is the world's second largest importer of oil behind the United States. Pollution levels are on the rise throughout the country and China tops the world in road accidents with about 450,000 accidents per year.

Now the world's second largest importer of oil, China is responsible for more than 40% of the world's growth in demand for oil in the last 5 years.

Pollution

China's cities are becoming more and more congested. Pollution is a growing serious threat to public health.

Safety

On Chinese roads, "might makes right." Bigger vehicles always have the right of way.

Lowest on the pecking order of China's vehicular "food chain," pedestrians often take their lives into their own hands while crossing a road.

Though changes are planned for China's driver testing system, the vast majority of drivers obtain their license by performing a set of maneuvers on an enclosed obstacle course. Their first experience in actual road conditions happens only after obtaining their license. With an estimated 1,000 new drivers hitting the road in this manner every day in Beijing, Chinese drivers are considered to be some of the worst drivers in the world.

Chinese drivers have a propensity to drive in the middle of the road regardless of lane markers. Coupled with the fact that a yellow light is usually interpreted as a signal to speed up, this makes many intersections in China very dangerous places.

China's famous bicycle culture still pervades many of its cities. Alas, in Beijing and Shanghai, it is quickly being replaced by the booming car culture. More and more people prefer cars to bicycles.

While roads in and around urban centers are generally very good, roads in the countryside are often little more than pothole-ridden dirt tracks.

An unusual road hazard exists in the form of elderly people dashing in front of moving vehicles. This is done to separate themselves from evil spirits they think are attached to their bodies. These evil spirits are believed to then attach themselves to the occupants of the cars.

When iron prices soar on global commodities exchanges, manhole covers very often begin to disappear in alarming numbers.

Public Transportation

Getting onto any form of public transportation in a crowded place often requires pushing and shoving to get on board.

Don't be surprised if, while riding public transportation, someone offers you his or her seat. It's all part of your celebrity status as a foreign guest. It also reflects the high value placed on hospitality in China.

When riding a train in China, openhearted strangers frequently offer you food and try to engage you in conversation.

Chinese people tend to have the uncanny ability of being able to fall asleep anywhere and at any time of day. This is most apparent while riding on public transportation.

10

DO'S AND DON'TS

There are a number of behaviors Westerners engage in that Chinese people may find objectionable. It is a good idea to apprise oneself of these behaviors and to avoid them as much as possible. Also, there are a few basic differences in how one should conduct oneself in social situations. The following illustrations focus on some of the more common do's and don'ts when interacting with Chinese people.

The Western practice of kissing someone as a greeting is considered inappropriate and much too forward. Don't do it.

If you happen to be a tall person, some Chinese people may feel a little intimidated by your height. When possible, try to lessen this effect, maybe by sitting on a chair or standing on a lower step of a staircase.

Don't forget, just because a Chinese person doesn't speak English, it doesn't mean they're deaf. Don't shout if you're having trouble being understood.

The Western informal practice of addressing someone on a first name basis is inappropriate in Chinese culture. It is best to use "Mister" or "Miss" when referring to yourself or to others. Better yet, if someone has a professional title (e.g., "Doctor", "Director"), by all means use it.

Friendly roughhousing is generally frowned upon and may be interpreted as aggression.

Using excessive hand motions while talking may be a great source of bewilderment for many Chinese people.

Avoid pointing at someone while talking. It may be interpreted as hostility.

Never assume that the locals can't speak English. You may end up saying something to embarrass yourself.

Try to avoid using exaggerative speech, especially common slang. Most Chinese people won't understand you.

Using idiomatic language is guaranteed to lead to misunderstandings.

It is considered rude to complain. Especially avoid complaining about China or aspects of its culture.

When giving someone a gift, always use two hands. Also, expect the person to decline the gift three or more times. This is the polite way of accepting a gift in China. Therefore, you must be insistent. Failure to persevere in your offer will be interpreted as a lack of sincerity on your part. The same rules apply when offering someone food or drinks.

A bit of fragrance clings to the hand that gives flowers.

—Chinese proverb

Inappropriate gifts include: 1) Clocks: a reminder of the passing of time and one's inevitable demise. 2) Knives or anything sharp: a symbol that you desire to sever the relationship. 3) Cut flowers: associated with funerals. 4) Handkerchiefs: associated with funerals and crying.

When accepting a compliment, avoid responding with "Thank you." This is considered arrogant or perhaps vain. The polite way to accept praise is to deny the veracity of the compliment and remain humble.

Chinese people often respond to a compliment by denying it with an opposite statement.

When being treated in a restaurant or going to someone's home, never pour your own drinks. Allow your host to do it. If you do happen to feel thirsty and feel shy about asking for more beverage, feel free to pour yourself a drink—but only after topping up the glasses of those around you.

Drinking soup from a bowl and making slurping sounds are both perfectly acceptable when eating in China.

When taking a break from eating, never plant your chopsticks in your food so they stand up. It resembles incense sticks in a censer used while praying for one's dead ancestors—very inappropriate at the dinner table.

When picking your teeth after a meal, the proper procedure is to cover your mouth with your other hand. Not doing so is considered extremely rude. It is akin to picking one's nose in public in Western culture.

Never agree when a Chinese person makes a self-deprecating comment. In fact, be sure to disagree wholeheartedly. In China, self-deprecating comments are expressions of modesty and indicative of a good upbringing.

When being treated to a meal, always be sure to leave a little bit of food on your plate when you're done eating. If you don't, your host may feel that you have not been properly fed. This reflects poorly on his or her ability as a host and can result in a loss of face.

Typical Western assertiveness is usually interpreted as rudeness or hostile aggression.

Blowing one's nose in public is considered crude and unrefined.

Public displays of affection (PDA) between members of the opposite sex are generally frowned upon and best avoided.

If you are ever in a situation where you are being applauded, it is appropriate for you to also clap—though not too forcefully.

Follow the local custom when you go to a foreign place.

—Chinese proverb

11

DOING BUSINESS IN CHINA

There are two main groups of Western professionals who tend to have dealings in China. They are English teachers and business people. Of these two groups, business people are most in need of cross-cultural training. In China, social missteps can often lead to serious consequences. If an English teacher commits a social blunder and gets fired, it is relatively easy to find another teaching job. However, if a business person commits a similar faux pas, it could result in the termination of a business deal or relationship and the resulting potential irretrievable loss of revenue. A clear understanding of Chinese customs can help one avoid negative outcomes resulting from cultural misunderstandings.

The following illustrations focus on some of the nuances of navigating China's business culture. There is also a section on Chinese negotiation tactics. Understanding these tactics in advance of any business negotiation can be helpful in devising effective counter-strategies. Reading as many books as possible on Chinese culture and business practices is also highly recommended. Consult the bibliography at the back of this book to get started.

When doing business in China, your goals and your Chinese partner's goals may be at odds with one another. Doubtless, making a profit is important to all parties concerned. Sometimes, though, Chinese interests also lie in developing the nation and contributing to the country's modernization drive. This consideration may sometimes take precedence over the goal of making profits. This may lead to a business relationship of "sharing the same bed but having different dreams."

If you must play, decide on three things at the start:
the rules of the game, the stakes, and the quitting time.

—Chinese proverb

Sometimes trying to get hold of someone on the telephone may seem like having to run an obstacle course. Before getting through to the person you want to talk to, you may have to go through a number of underlings. Each one is likely to ask you a series of questions regarding your name, the reason for your call, and so on....

When trying to get someone on the phone, it is best to refer to yourself as your company name. For example: "Hello, I am Acme Widget Company. May I speak to so and so?" Your personal name will mean nothing to the receptionist and may likely lead to confusion or a failure to get through.

Chinese business people are notorious for not answering their e-mails in a timely fashion—if at all. Faxes, telephone calls and regular mail are usually more likely to generate some kind of response.

The hours between noon and 2:00 PM are reserved for lunch—followed by a long nap. It's a good idea not to waste your time trying to conduct business during these hours, whether in person or by phone.

When receiving someone's business card, it is extremely rude to simply stuff it into a pocket without reading it first. The proper etiquette involves receiving it with both hands, taking time to study it a little and maybe reading the person's name and title out loud. Failure to do so may result in a loss of face for the person handing you their card. It demonstrates a lack of interest in that person.

Never hand out your business cards in a perfunctory way. It shows a lack of respect, both for yourself and for the person receiving the card.

Many businesses in China are family affairs with key positions occupied by close relatives and family members. Whereas nepotism is generally a dirty word in Western culture, in China it is normal business practice.

When first encountering a Chinese business negotiation team, never make assumptions based on appearance about someone's rank in the team. You never can tell. The team leader may in fact be the poorly dressed individual wearing white socks and black shoes sitting observantly away from the action.

When entering a room as part of a negotiation team, Chinese negotiators will always assume that the first person to enter the room is the team leader.

The seat of honor in a meeting room or at a dinner table is always the seat immediately to the right of the host. The primary host always sits in the chair furthest away from and facing the entrance with his or her back to the wall.

A Chinese nod does not always necessarily indicate agreement. Usually it merely indicates that the person is listening and paying attention to what you are saying.

The concept of a civil service was invented in China hundreds of years ago. It is one of the main factors that contributed to China's long continuous civilization. Numerous imperial dynasties have risen and fallen throughout China's long history. All throughout, the Chinese bureaucracy was always present—holding things together and keeping society running.

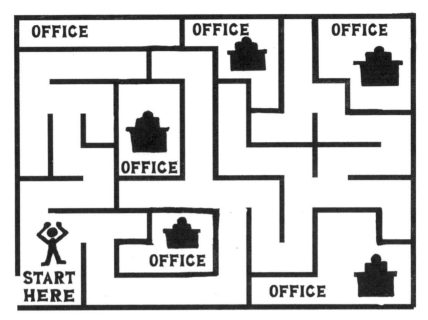

Chinese bureaucracy is vast and cumbersome. For many people, it seems very much like an impenetrable maze. Furthermore, based in a society prone to an "us and them" mentality, interdepartmental cooperation is virtually nonexistent.

Most government offices are run like personal kingdoms. Department heads revel in their godlike status no matter how insignificant their particular office happens to be.

Large numbers of bureaucrats enjoy nothing more than sitting around all day reading the newspaper and drinking tea. Most dealings with government offices move along at a snail's pace.

Bribery at all levels of government is highly illegal though still very common. Most civil servants are seriously underpaid yet are crucial to granting approvals and performing other vital bureaucratic functions. They sometimes rely on alternative sources of income to supplement their salaries. Be careful though. Just because you're a foreigner, it doesn't mean you're above the law. If caught trying to bribe a government official, expect legal trouble probably requiring more bribery in order to avoid prison.

Within business and bureaucratic hierarchies, blame tends to flow downwards. The lower one's rank, the bigger share of the blame one must bear.

It takes little effort to watch a man carry a load.

—Chinese proverb

Afraid of making mistakes and having to bear responsibility for potential problems, most underlings in business and bureaucratic hierarchies tend to avoid making decisions. Ultimately, group leaders in any management structure are often mired in petty minutiae passed up the line.

Business Negotiations

Business negotiations in China typically take place in a designated meeting room. The leader of the Chinese team invariably sits in the chair farthest from and facing the entrance. The foreign team leader usually sits in the seat of honor to the immediate right of the Chinese team leader. Chinese negotiation teams tend to be quite large and very well prepared. During negotiations, Chinese team members usually take copious amounts of notes on the proceedings. It is wise to have someone on your team do the same. Also, having a good interpreter on your team is indispensable. During the negotiation process, always address the Chinese team leader and try to avoid focusing your attention on the interpreter.

Many people in China, particularly business people, are well versed in Sun Tzu's *The Art of War*, a 5th-century-BCE treatise on military tactics. This book focuses on cunning and deception as primary strategies in war. It is interesting to note that in China, a deity named Guang Gung is the patron god of both business and war.

The Western view of business is generally that of a game or a sport. In addition to a warlike approach to commerce in China, business relationships are also viewed somewhat like a marriage. All's fair in love and war.

In business, Chinese negotiation teams typically prepare well in advance. At the outset, they arrive at the table with reams of meticulously prepared information regarding their company, the deal under consideration, technical data, etc.... It's a good idea for foreign entrepreneurs to do the same.

On the initial day of negotiations, do not expect to discuss business. Instead, be prepared to deliver an introductory speech replete with generalized platitudes and garden-variety clichés celebrating the upcoming round of negotiations.

After the initial meeting, all subsequent meetings will usually begin with a fair amount of small talk designed to set the mood and establish a comfortable relaxed atmosphere.

Nothing is more difficult than the art of maneuvering for advantageous positions.

—Sun Tzu, **The Art of War**

Chinese Negotiation Tactics

There are several unique tactics Chinese negotiators use when dealing with foreigners. Being aware of these tactics may help to alleviate any pressure you may feel to make unnecessary concessions while you negotiate.

Chinese people seem to be more comfortable with silence in groups compared to their Western counterparts. Silence is also sometimes used as a negotiation tactic. In business meetings, avoid making concessions during any pregnant pauses simply as a means of breaking the silence. Instead, smile, relax and enjoy the quiet time.

Be extremely subtle, even to the point of formlessness.
Be extremely mysterious, even to the point of soundlessness.
Thereby you can be the director of the opponent's fate.

—Sun Tzu, The Art of War

Feigning anger is also a common Chinese tactic during negotiations. Generally, you are being tested for any weaknesses. It is best not to react at all and to put on your best poker face.

Drinking alcohol and making round after round of toasts are fundamental to Chinese business practices. Try to stay as sober as possible during these male bonding rituals. Also be careful what you say. You will most certainly be held to any concessions you happen to make while inebriated.

Making you feel guilty for China's lack of prosperity relative to the West is also a common negotiation strategy.

If you happen to be from one of the countries that exploited the Chinese people during the 19th and 20th centuries, expect a guilt trip to be laid upon you for your country's past transgressions.

Chinese companies are notorious for playing one foreign company off one or more other foreign rivals. It is even possible for a Chinese company to simultaneously carry on negotiations with two foreign competitors in adjacent meeting rooms.

Another strategy involves refusing to take "no" for an answer. No matter what, stick to your guns.

Business negotiations in China often seem to drag on forever. Chinese negotiators generally love to rehash details over and over again. Sometimes it is simply because the process has been stalled for some reason. Other times, it is a reflection of a holistic rather than a linear approach to problem solving.

Post-Negotiations

It is important to note that the negotiation process does not necessarily end with the signing of a contract. The Chinese perception of legal contracts is very different from the Western view. More emphasis is placed on what is said than on what is written. The written contract merely expresses a desire by both parties to do business with one another. In reality, negotiations never really end. If one party decides on the need for a change at any time, everything is up for discussion. For foreign entrepreneurs, this is perhaps the most frustrating aspect of China's business culture.

Once a deal is concluded, you will notice that your Chinese counterparts will "sign" the contract in red ink with a stamp called a name chop. Name chops are used throughout China for all official business requiring a personal signature. This includes making bank transactions or selling property.

After perhaps months or even years of negotiations, most contracts are generally stowed away in a filing cabinet and quickly forgotten. In China, contracts are basically seen as mere letters of intent to form a business partnership. The most important aspect of the negotiation process is the opportunity to form meaningful and long lasting relationships.

Don't open a shop unless you like to smile.

—Chinese proverb

When a business dispute arises, citing previously agreed upon contractual provisions should only be used as a last resort. In China, bringing up the contract at the first sign of trouble is analogous to threatening a spouse with divorce for squeezing a toothpaste tube in the middle, rather than at the bottom. Hard feelings are certain to arise. It may even prove to be a deal breaker. It is best to try and work things out through continued discussions rather than make reference to the contract.

He who strikes the first blow admits he's lost the argument.

—Chinese proverb

BEAUTIFUL CHINA

With its long history and being a large country of great diversity, China has much to offer as a travel destination. The most popular spots in China are Beijing, Shanghai, Hong Kong, Guilin, and of course the Great Wall, which snakes across more than 6,700 km (4,160 miles) of the Chinese countryside. Most impressive!

Bibliography

Travel

Lonely Planet: China. Damian Harper, Steve Fallon, Katja Gaskell, Julie Grundvig, Carolyn Heller, Thomas Huhti, Bradley Mayhew, Christopher Pitts. Lonely Planet Publications, Hawthorn, Victoria, Australia, 2005.

Lonely Planet: Mandarin Phrasebook. Justin Rudelson, Charles Qin. Footscray. Victoria, Australia, 2000.

Lonely Planet: Taiwan. Robert Storey. Lonely Planet Publications, Hawthorn, Victoria, Australia, 1998.

The Rough Guide to China. Written and researched by David Leffman, Simon Lewis and Jeremy Atiyah. Additional contributions by Simon Foster, Travis Klingberg, Mike Meyer and Xiaoshan Sun. Rough Guides, New York, London, Delhi, 2005.

General

Asian Power and Politics: The Cultural Dimensions of Authority. Lucian W. Pye with Mary W. Pye. The Belknap Press of Harvard University Press, Cambridge, Massachusetts, 1985.

China, Inc.: How the Rise of the Next Superpower Challenges America and the World. Ted C. Fishman. Scribner, New York, 2006.

Culture Shock! China. Kevin Sinclair and Iris Wong Po-yee. Graphic Arts Center Publishing Company, Portland, Oregon, 2004

Culture Shock! Taiwan. Chris and Ling Li Bates. Graphic Arts Center Publishing Company, Portland, Oregon, 1995

Will the Boat Sink the Water? : The Life of China's Peasants. Chen Guidi and Wu Chuntao, translated from Chinese by Zhu Hong. Public Affairs, New York, 2006

Business

Chinese Business Etiquette: A Guide to Protocol, Manners, and Culture in the People's Republic of China. Scott D. Seligman. Warner Business Books, New York, 1999.

Chinese Business Etiquette and Culture. Kevin Bucknall. Boson Books, Raleigh, N.C., 2002.

Harvard Business Review on Doing Business in China. Harvard Business School Press, Boston, 2004.

Made in China: What Western Managers Can Learn from Trailblazing Chinese Entrepreneurs. Donald N. Sull with Yong Wang. Harvard Business School Press, Boston, 2005.

One Billion Customers: Lessons from the Front Lines of Doing Business in China. James McGregor. The Free Press, New York, 2005.

INDEX

Pierre Ostrowski is a Canadian who left the frozen North for Asia in 1996. He has spent his time in Asia teaching English, studying languages and traveling as much as possible. He studied Chinese at Providence University in Taichung, Taiwan. In addition, he spent his leisure hours studying Chinese cuisine and perfecting his Ma Pou Doufu recipe. Although he has traveled to over twenty countries in Asia and elsewhere, some of his fondest memories are related to China. As far as he's concerned, there's nothing quite as sublime as sitting on a remote section of the Great Wall of China and watching it snake off into infinity over rolling hills of green…the perfect Chinese moment.

Gwen Penner, a graduate of the University of Manitoba's Bachelor of Fine Arts (Honours) program, is the recipient of numerous awards in painting, drawing and printmaking. She has spent the last several years living in Asia. An inquisitive person, Gwen has a profound understanding of Chinese culture, and her insight into the intricacies of Chinese culture comes through in the many subtle nuances she incorporates into her illustrations. She is fond of traveling throughout China and talking with the locals to learn their interpretations of what it means to be Chinese.